THREE
DIMENSIONS
OF MAN

Ernest Addo

Copyright © 2015 Ernest Addo

Published by Little Books Publications, United Kingdom

First edition 2015

Email Ernest Addo:

ernest.addo1@yahoo.com

Find out more about Ernest Addo at:

www.facebook.com/LivingJesusTabernacle

ISBN: 978-0-9932250-0-0

Printed by Polestar UK Print Limited (Wheatons)

Dedication

I first and foremost dedicate this book to the
Almighty God for saving me through His Son
Jesus Christ and for giving me the greatest
privilege and honour to serve Him with my life.

I also dedicate this book to
Bishop Dag Heward-Mills.
Thank you for training me in the ministry and
inspiring me to serve the Lord.

Contents

Preface

As I have pastored God's people over the years, I have noticed a great problem in the kingdom of God. Many believers do not really understand what it means to be a Christian. Because of this, they are not deeply rooted in Christ. As a young man, I used to attend church regularly. I used to sing, dance and give offerings but I did not know the Lord. I did not completely understand who I was in Christ or even how to properly worship my Creator. Like many others, I was just a church goer.

The sad reality is that there are churches filled with baby Christians who simply do not know the Lord. Believers have not been taught simple truths on how to walk with God. This leaves them open to spiritual attacks and even send some to marching on the broad way to hell. The truth is we spend just a few hours a week in church so what we do outside of church greatly affects our Christian walk. This is why the Bible encourages each of us to *"work out your own salvation with fear and trembling" (Philippians 2:12)*. You see, a large part of basic Christian living depends on the believer, not the pastor.

Let me share with you what prompted me to write this book. I went to church one Sunday after fasting and praying for two weeks. As a result, I was expecting the power of God to descend mightily upon the congregation. The power of God did indeed move mightily and many people were delivered. But it suddenly occurred to me that the congregation lacked His word for growth. This realisation made me understand how important the word of God is in making us solid Christians.

As a growing church, the members were getting used to the power of God and they always came to church expecting a move of God. We certainly need the power of God in our lives but His word is even more vital for our Christian maturity. Christians cannot live on His mighty power alone!

God wants large churches! Large churches means more saved souls! But without a personal relationship with the Lord, precious souls will not be established in Christ. I was prompted by the Holy Spirit to start teaching the church the basics of Christian living and how to walk with the Lord. It is for this very reason that this book is now in your hands.

When God created Adam, He placed him in the Garden of Eden for him to dress it. Likewise, God has put pastors in His church to dress His people for His coming. Pastors must rise up and stop playing games in the church. We must teach believers the truth if we are to perfect the saints for the coming of our Lord Jesus Christ.

Pastors, God is depending on us to prepare His bride for the marriage of the Lamb! We must be careful to do what the Lord has instructed us to do.

We must teach God's people how to walk with Him and not turn Christians into sign seekers, money seekers or people lusting for the things of the world. The Father's desire is that His churches are filled with Christians who truly know Him and have a personal relationship with Him.

Perhaps you picked up this book because you desire a deeper relationship with Jesus Christ. I pray that as you read this book, the Holy Spirit will open your eyes to truly know the Lord and that you will walk with Him in spirit and in truth in every area of your life.

In the mighty name of Jesus Christ, AMEN!

And the very God of peace sanctify you wholly; and I pray God your whole spirit and soul and body be preserved blameless unto the coming of our Lord Jesus Christ.

1 Thessalonians 5: 23

Chapter 1

Man is a Three Dimensional Being

How do you define a human being? We could start by saying that humans are intelligent beings. Just by looking around us we can see that mankind has been able to invent many things from aircrafts to cars and computers. We have designed houses, bridges, roads and many more amazing things in this world. Intelligence and creativity are both aspects of God's character. The bible says in **Genesis 1:26** that we are created in the likeness and image of God the Father, God the Son and God the Holy Spirit.

We can also say that humans are superior beings. Mankind is so superior that we are able to capture the wildest animals and cage them in a zoo. We are able to travel across oceans, dig deep into the earth and even fly to the moon. Because God has created us like Himself, His characteristics of dominion and authority have also been imparted to man.

Unfortunately even with all these capabilities, it is clear that mankind has gradually lost its higher God-given state and become worse than animals. How has this happened? It is because many people do not know who they are. They do not know what they must do whilst on earth or where they are going at the end of life.

But there is good news! The bible reveals the most important definition of a human being. The word of God defines every human being as having a spirit, soul and body. We are first and foremost three dimensional eternal beings!

And the very God of peace sanctify you wholly; and I pray God your whole spirit and soul and body be preserved blameless unto the coming of our Lord Jesus Christ.
1 Thessalonians 5: 23

This scripture in **1 Thessalonians** clearly explains that mankind is three dimensional. Every human being has a spirit and a soul and is living in a container called the body. When you become born again in Christ, you realise that you are more than just a piece of meat. You are an eternal being with a destiny, a purpose and authority! This is why humans are very different from animals. When animals die they are eaten but when humans die they are buried far away from society. If death meant the end of man and all there is to him, it would be a sad story indeed!

I believe that ignorance is a great killer in this world. Lack of knowledge causes many to perish in vain. For instance, if you do not know that touching electricity with water kills and you do so, you will die as a result of ignorance. Meanwhile, it could have been prevented through knowledge and teaching that touching water with electricity kills. In a similar way, Christians must be taught about the three aspects of man so that they can truly walk in spirit and truth. Teaching brings knowledge and understanding. By understanding how to possess their spirit, soul and body; Christians will be built up, rooted in Christ and preserved blameless until His coming.

Therefore if any man be in Christ, he is a new creature: old things are passed away; behold, all things are become new.

2 Corinthians 5:17

Chapter 2

The Spirit of Man

As I mentioned in the previous chapter, man is three dimensional. The bible says that every human being is a spirit, they have a soul and their spirit lives in a container called the body. Therefore, the real **you** is not your physical body. The real **you** is your spirit and your spirit is a tenant in your body. Apostle Paul referred to the spirit of man as the *inward* man or the *inner* man. This is because the spirit of man cannot be seen with the natural eye; it is encrypted in the body. Many scriptures speak of this *hidden* man.

For which cause we faint not; but though our outward man perish, yet the *inward* man is renewed day by day.

2 Corinthians 4:16

For I delight in the law of God after the *inward* man.

Romans 7:22

But let it be the *hidden* man of the heart, in that which is not corruptible, even the ornament of a meek and quiet spirit, which is in the sight of God of great price.

1 Peter 3:4

That he would grant you, according to the riches of his glory, to be strengthened with might by his Spirit in the *inner* man.

Ephesians 3:16

When God formed man from the dust, He breathed into man the breath of life. The very breath of God created the spirit of man and gave life to the body. This is why the spirit of man is an eternal spirit because it comes directly from the eternal God. Hallelujah!

And the Lord God formed man of the dust of the ground, and breathed into his nostrils the breath of life; and man became a living soul.

Genesis 2:7

The Spirit of God hath made me, and the breath of the Almighty hath given me life.

Job 33:4

The spirit of man lives forever because God created man in His own image and God lives forever. One day your spirit will hand in its tenancy notice to your body and leave to go to its eternal home which will be either in heaven or in hell. We see an example of this in everyday life when people move homes.

Over the years, I have lived in various houses in London but I no longer live in them. The real **me** has left those houses and is now living in my current home. This is precisely what happens with the spirit of man and the body. The word of God gives us an example of this truth with the Rich Man and Lazarus in **Luke chapter 16**. Both of these men were dead and yet they were alive. This is incredible!

There was a certain rich man, which was clothed in purple and fine linen, and fared sumptuously every day: And there was a certain beggar named Lazarus, which was laid at his gate, full of sores, And desiring to be fed with the crumbs which fell from the rich man's table: moreover the dogs came and licked his sores.

And it came to pass, that the beggar died, and was carried by the angels into Abraham's bosom: the rich man also died, and was buried; And in hell he lift up his eyes, being in torments, and seeth Abraham afar off, and Lazarus in his bosom. And he cried and said, Father Abraham, have mercy on me, and send Lazarus that he may dip the tip of his finger in water, and cool my tongue; for I am tormented in this flame.

But Abraham said, Son, remember that thou in thy lifetime receiveth thy good things, and likewise Lazarus evil things: but now he is comforted, and thou art tormented. And beside all this, between us and you there is a great gulf fixed: so that they which would pass from hence to you cannot; neither can they pass to us that would come from thence.

Then he said, I pray thee therefore, father, that thou wouldest send him to my father's house: For I have five brethren; that he may testify unto them, lest they also come into this place of torment. Abraham saith unto him, They have Moses and the prophets; let them hear them. And he said, Nay, father Abraham: but if one went unto them from the dead, they will repent. And he said unto him, If they hear not Moses and the prophets, neither will they be persuaded, though one rose from the dead.

Luke 16:19-31

You can see from the above passage of scripture that the Rich Man was dead. So how could he speak, taste and see? How could he be thirsty and wanting water to drink? How could he feel the torments in hell? This clearly shows us that his real self, *his spirit*, had only left his physical body but he was very much alive. His spirit still had all the characteristics of a man and could speak and feel. I tell you the truth, the spirit of man never dies, so we must prepare it for the coming of the Lord Jesus Christ.

This is why salvation is the greatest gift we have received through Jesus Christ. I mentioned previously that mankind has lost its God-given attributes and become worse than animals. But thanks be to God for salvation! Through his precious son Jesus Christ, we can be born again with a new eternal spirit! In order to truly understand this wonderful gift, let us look at mankind before salvation and after receiving salvation.

The Spirit of Man before Salvation

In the beginning God created man as an eternal spirit with a soul and body. The spirit of man was in direct union and fellowship with God until Adam and Eve sinned in the Garden of Eden. As soon as Adam and Eve sinned, their eternal spirits were cut off from God.

And they heard the voice of the Lord God walking in the garden in the cool of the day: and Adam and his wife hid themselves from the presence of the Lord God amongst the trees of the garden.

Genesis 3:8

God had warned Adam that the day that he ate the fruit of a particular tree he would die. However this did not mean a physical death but a spiritual death. Sin causes separation from God and can end in spiritual death. Since sin entered into the world, man has been hiding and running away from God. Mankind has gone its own way, doing all kinds of evil things.

All we like sheep have gone astray; we have turned every one to his own way; and the Lord hath laid on him the iniquity of us all.

Isaiah 53:6

Spiritual death is the state of an unsaved spirit. An unsaved spirit does not believe in Jesus Christ and is dominated by the flesh and is subject to the works of the flesh. An unsaved man therefore carries and displays the nature of satan.

Now the works of the flesh are manifest, which are these; Adultery, fornication, uncleanness, lasciviousness, Idolatry, witchcraft, hatred, variance, emulations, wrath, strife, seditions, heresies, Envyings, murders, drunkenness, revellings, and such like:

Of the which I tell you before, as I have also told you in time past, that they which do such things shall not inherit the kingdom of God.

Galatians 5:19-21

The works of the flesh show the true nature of the unsaved spirit of man. He is wicked and full of evil. **Jeremiah 17:9** tells us that the spirit of a man who is not saved is desperately wicked. The word "heart" in this scripture means *spirit*. This helps us to understand why there is so much wickedness and atrocities in the world because the works of the flesh are manifest.

Many people argue about salvation; what it is and if they even need it. To put it simply, without salvation, our spirit is dead and we cannot hear from God. Without salvation, we can only do evil. Without salvation, we are all heading to hell. This is why we must be saved! You can never be good enough for heaven except through the blood of Jesus Christ.

But we are all as an unclean thing, and all our righteousness are as filthy rags; and we all do fade as a leaf; and our iniquities, like the wind, have taken us away.

Isaiah 64:6

God has already paid the heavy price by sending his son Jesus Christ to die for our sins. We did not ask Him to do this for us but He did it anyway. He first loved us, He thought about us and He did not want us to burn in hell fire. That is why He sent His precious Son Jesus Christ to become flesh and dwell among us. Anyone who believes in Him and calls on His name shall be saved. Hallelujah!

But God commendeth his love toward us, in that, while we were yet sinners, Christ died for us.

Romans 5:8

The Spirit of Man after Salvation

The spirit of man is saved by believing and confessing Jesus Christ as your Lord and Saviour.

That if thou shalt confess with thy mouth the Lord Jesus, and shalt believe in thine heart that God hath raised him from the dead, thou shalt be saved. For with the heart man believeth unto righteousness; and with the mouth confession is made unto salvation.

Romans 10:9-10

I tell you the truth; you do not get saved by confessing your sins. You do not get saved by baptism. You do not get saved by your good works or deeds. There is only one way you can be saved. That is by believing and confessing Jesus Christ as your Lord and Saviour.

To be "born again" means to be *re-birthed*, *re-made* or *recreated* again. Your old nature is replaced with a new nature.

Therefore if any man be in Christ, he is a new creature: old things are passed away; behold, all things are become new.

2 Corinthians 5:17

When a person becomes born again, their dead spirit is recreated by God and given a new life reconciled back to God. Nicodemus, a ruler of the Jews, did not understand when Jesus told him to be born again. He thought that Jesus meant he should go back into his mother's womb in order to be brought into this world again. Jesus actually meant that he must be given birth to spiritually. The body does not become born again; it is the spirit that is born again.

Jesus answered and said unto him, Verily, verily, I say unto thee, Except a man be born again, he cannot see the kingdom of God.

Nicodemus saith unto him, How can a man be born when he is old? can he enter the second time into his mother's womb, and be born?

Jesus answered, Verily, verily, I say unto thee, Except a man be born of water and of the Spirit, he cannot enter into the kingdom of God.

That which is born of the flesh is flesh; and that which is born of the Spirit is spirit. Marvel not that I said unto thee, Ye must be born again.

John 3:3-7

Jesus was telling Nicodemus that although his parents gave birth to him physically, he must now be born into the kingdom of God spiritually. Spiritual birth gives man a change of heart or *spirit*. The wicked heart of man is changed by God and when this happens they become a new person. Their old, wicked ways are now forgiven and their life becomes brand new like that of a newborn baby.

And Jesus, when he was baptized, went up straightway out of the water: and, lo, the heavens were opened unto him, and he saw the Spirit of God descending like a dove, and lighting upon him.

Matthew 3:16

Chapter 3

Christian Water Baptism

New believers tend to confuse being born again with water baptism. They think it is the same as being born again. However, if a person is not born again and they get baptised, that does not make the person saved. That person has only been washed with water and nothing spiritual has taken place in their heart. Salvation is of the heart and water baptism alone does not reach the heart. After all we bath everyday!

I was baptised and confirmed while in secondary school. The only reason why I decided to do both baptism and confirmation was so I never had to do them again. But I was wrong. I was wrong because I was not saved before baptism and confirmation. So after the baptism and confirmation, there was no change in my life. I did not know the Lord; neither did I have a relationship with Him. I was an unsaved soul washed with drinking water.

But two years after this event, I received the Lord as my Saviour into my heart and became truly born again. I was then baptised again, but this time, I felt the Holy Spirit on my life whilst I was coming out of the water. I was a born again, Holy Spirit filled, tongue speaking believer.

Jesus said, *"Except a man is born of the water and of the Spirit he cannot enter into the kingdom of God" (John 3:5).* The word "water" in this verse has nothing to do with baptism but it is talking about the word of God which is able to save our souls. We become born again by the word. Read it for yourself.

Being born again, not of corruptible seed, but of incorruptible, by the word of God, which liveth and abideth for ever.

1 Peter 1:23

We therefore do not become born again or get saved by water baptism. **Ephesians 5:26** makes this even clearer as it refers to the word of God as water.

That he might sanctify and cleanse it with the washing of water by the word.

Ephesians 5:26

You can now understand that if you are baptised with water and you are not first saved by the word of God, then you are deceiving yourself to think that you are saved. Water baptism is symbolic of our death and resurrection with Jesus Christ. It is also our public declaration that we are saved. The lowering of the person in water signifies our death with Jesus Christ and the raising of the person out of the water symbolises our resurrection with Jesus Christ.

Therefore we are buried with him by baptism into death: that like as Christ was raised up from the dead by the glory of the Father, even so we also should walk in newness of life. For if we have been planted together in the likeness of his death, we shall be also in the likeness of his resurrection.

Romans 6:4-5

The Correct Form of Baptism

The word "baptism" comes from the Greek word "baptiso" which means *whelm* or to *fully submerge*. It does not mean sprinkling of water. As I mentioned earlier, the baptism that I did in secondary school was sprinkling of water and it made no difference in my life.

Let's get it right. We are imitators of Jesus Christ and He is our best example in all aspects of our Christian life. We must therefore allow the word of God to guide us and not follow the traditions of men. Jesus himself was baptised by John the Baptist and He was immersed totally in water.

Then cometh Jesus from Galilee to Jordan unto John, to be baptized of him. But John forbad him, saying, I have need to be baptized of thee, and comest thou to me?

And Jesus answering said unto him, Suffer it to be so now: for thus it becometh us to fulfil all righteousness. Then he suffered him. And Jesus, when he was baptized, went up straightway out of the water: and, lo, the heavens were opened unto him, and he saw the Spirit of God descending like a dove, and lighting upon him:

And lo a voice from heaven, saying, This is my beloved Son, in whom I am well pleased.

Matthew 3:13-17

In the above passage of scripture, you can see that Jesus came out of the River Jordan. Therefore, He was fully immersed in the water. Jesus even came out of the water praying. Now in the mouth of two or three shall every word be established so I will give a second example.

Apart from the example of Jesus' baptism, the disciple named Philip also baptised the Ethiopian eunuch. In this amazing passage of scripture in **Acts chapter 8**, the Ethiopian eunuch requested that Philip baptise him. But look at what Philip said to him. Philip said, *"If thou believest with all thine heart"*. The Ethiopian eunuch was born again **before** being baptised by complete immersion in the water. Read it for yourself.

And the angel of the Lord spake unto Philip, saying, Arise, and go toward the south unto the way that goeth down from Jerusalem unto Gaza, which is desert. And he arose and went: and, behold, a man of Ethiopia, an eunuch of great authority under Candace queen of the Ethiopians, who had the charge of all her treasure, and had come to Jerusalem for to worship, Was returning, and sitting in his chariot read Esaias the prophet.

Then the Spirit said unto Philip, Go near, and join thyself to this chariot. And Philip ran thither to him, and heard him read the prophet Esaias, and said, Understandest thou what thou readest? And he said, How can I, except some man should guide me? And he desired Philip that he would come

up and sit with him. The place of the scripture which he read was this, He was led as a sheep to the slaughter; and like a lamb dumb before his shearer, so opened he not his mouth: In his humiliation his judgment was taken away: and who shall declare his generation? for his life is taken from the earth.

And the eunuch answered Philip, and said, I pray thee, of whom speaketh the prophet this? of himself, or of some other man? Then Philip opened his mouth, and began at the same scripture, and preached unto him Jesus. And as they went on their way, they came unto a certain water: and the eunuch said, See, here is water; what doth hinder me to be baptized? And Philip said, *If thou believest with all thine heart*, thou mayest. And he answered and said, I believe that Jesus Christ is the Son of God.

And he commanded the chariot to stand still: and they went down both into the water, both Philip and the eunuch; and he baptized him. And when they were come up out of the water, the Spirit of the Lord caught away Philip, that the eunuch saw him no more: and he went on his way rejoicing. But Philip was found at Azotus: and passing through he preached in all the cities, till he came to Caesarea.

Acts 8:26-40

Pastors, if you are not close to any sea or river where you can baptise your members, you can also do so in a swimming pool. The most important thing is to do the baptism as Jesus did. He was baptised by being fully immersed in the water.

Wherefore lay apart all filthiness and superfluity of naughtiness, and receive with meekness the engrafted word, which is able to save your souls.

James 1:21

Chapter 4

The Soul of Man

The second dimension of man is the soul. The soul is a result of the coming together of the spirit of man and the body of man. The soul of man is the invisible part of man that enables him to think, to reason and to feel. In other words, the soul of man can also be called the mind of the person.

And the Lord God formed man of the dust of the ground, and breathed into his nostrils the breath of life, and man became a living soul.

Genesis 2:7

When a person becomes born again, their spirit is saved but the soul needs to be renewed. After you have given your life to Jesus Christ, your soul can still have the same feelings, thoughts and evil desires you had when you were unsaved. It is therefore important that every believer feeds on the word of God daily in order to transform and save their soul. The word of God is the only hope for the soul's salvation.

Wherefore lay apart all filthiness and superfluity of naughtiness, and receive with meekness the engrafted word, which is able to save your souls.

James 1:21

The law of the LORD is perfect, converting the soul: the testimony of the LORD is sure, making wise the simple.

Psalm 19:7

We know that the spirit is converted by accepting Jesus as Lord and Saviour but these scriptures tell us that the soul is converted by the transforming word of God.

The soul is a great asset to the believer. Whatever you entertain in the mind, once it filters into the heart, it is acted out. With your mind you can think of both good and evil. True transformation comes when the mind of the Christian is renewed to think on the right things. But this transformation does not take place until the individual begins to feed on the word of God.

And be not conformed to this world: but be ye transformed by the renewing of your mind, that ye may prove what is that good, and acceptable, and perfect, will of God.

Romans 12:2

The Mind is the Battle Ground

An untransformed mind will destroy a Christian. The kingdom of darkness knows this and that is why the soul often becomes a stronghold for satan. The devil continually brings evil thoughts to our minds and if we feed on such thoughts, we will eventually act on them. This strategy often leads Christians into sin. The devil thrives on the power of suggestion. By suggesting things to your mind, he brings thoughts that will not ordinarily occur to you. For example, the devil spoke to Eve, *"Yea, hath God said, Ye shall not eat of every tree of the garden?"* *(Genesis 3:1)*. This suggestion landed Adam and Eve into sin.

Sometimes you wonder why tongue speaking, born again Christians have weird imaginations and lusts. Do not be surprised, the devil is playing with their minds!

For the weapons of our warfare are not carnal, but mighty through God to the pulling down of strongholds;

Casting down imaginations, and every high thing that exalteth itself against the knowledge of God, and bringing into captivity every thought to the obedience of Christ.

2 Corinthians 10:4-5

Renewing your Mind

The best way to fight this strategy is by renewing your mind. You must think on things which are pure, honest, lovely and of good report. This is what the word of God suggests for the transformation of the soul.

And the peace of God, which passeth all understanding, shall keep your hearts and minds through Christ Jesus.

Finally, brethren, whatsoever things are true, whatsoever things are honest, whatsoever things are just, whatsoever things are

pure, whatsoever things are lovely, whatsoever things are of good report; if there be any virtue, and if there be any praise, think on these things.

Philippians 4:7-8

Christians! We must renew our minds in every area and save our souls!

Our minds must be renewed about going to church. The word of God makes it clear that we should not forsake fellowshipping with the saints.

Not forsaking the assembling of ourselves together, as the manner of some is; but exhorting one another: and so much the more, as ye see the day approaching.

Hebrews 10:25

Most Christians only attend church on Sundays while some attend once a month, or once every three months or only at Christmas! This behaviour is exhibited by Christians whose minds are not renewed with the word of God. If you read God's word, your mind will be renewed about the power of fellowship.

Our minds must be renewed about giving. Some Christians think that pastors spend the church tithes and offerings and therefore they never give to the church. This type of thinking has made a lot of Christians poor as it is one of the main sources of blessings from the Lord. Some people even stop going to church because of this reason.

If only they would read and meditate on the word of God, their minds would be renewed. They would soon realise that it is to their own

The Soul of Man

personal benefit to give to the church in support of the gospel in order to be blessed by the Lord.

> **Bring ye all the tithes into the storehouse, that there may be meat in mine house, and prove me now herewith, saith the Lord of hosts, if I will not open you the windows of heaven, and pour you out a blessing, that there shall not be room enough to receive it.**
> **Malachi 3:10**

Another area that our minds must be renewed is marriage. A Christian must never marry an unbeliever. This simple truth which has not been learnt by countless born again Christians has sadly led many into bondage. The word of God is crystal clear on the matter.

> **Be ye not unequally yoked together with unbelievers: for what fellowship hath righteousness with unrighteousness? and what communion hath light with darkness?**
> **2 Corinthians 6:14**

I therefore urge every Christian to arm their minds with the word of God. Protect your mind from evil thoughts with the precious word of God. Resist the evil thoughts that flood your mind with the word and you will win the battle of the mind. Satan will actually flee from you. The fact that you are a Christian does not shield you from evil thoughts but the engrafted word is able to free your mind and help you to resist the devil.

> **Submit yourselves therefore to God. Resist the devil, and he will flee from you.**
> **James 4:7**

29

I beseech you therefore, brethren, by the mercies of God, that ye present your bodies a living sacrifice, holy, acceptable unto God, which is your reasonable service.

Romans 12:1

Chapter 5

The Body of Man

We now know that the spirit is saved by our Saviour Jesus Christ, and that the soul is renewed through His word. We will now learn about the third dimension, the salvation of the body. It is the duty of every Christian to keep their body under control in order to be free from sin. The scriptures below tell us that the Lord wants us to present our bodies as living sacrifice.

I beseech you therefore, brethren, by the mercies of God, that ye present your bodies a living sacrifice, holy, acceptable unto God, which is your reasonable service.

Romans 12:1

But I keep under my body, and bring it into subjection: lest that by any means, when I have preached to others, I myself should be a castaway.

1 Corinthians 9:27

This means it is our *reasonable* duty as Christians to ensure that we subject our bodies to the obedience of the word of God. Even Apostle Paul said that he kept his body under control so that he would not be a castaway. You see, it does not matter your spiritual position in Christ.

If you do not lead your body, it will lead you to hell. The body must be kept under control.

Mortify therefore your members which are upon the earth; fornication, uncleanness, inordinate affection, evil concupiscence, and covetousness, which is idolatry.

Colossians 3:5

The word "mortify" in **Colossians 3:5** comes from the Greek word "nekroo" which means: *to deaden, to subdue, to hold within limit or control, self-denial, check, crucify, discipline and to train.* The word of God urges us to *train*, to *subdue* and to *crucify* the body in order to be free from sin. This is because the body is still the same after salvation and therefore capable of every form of evil under the sun.

This is the reason why a person can receive Jesus Christ today and still continue in sin the following day. The body is still the same and it must be controlled with the word of God.

The Holy Spirit gave me an astonishing revelation, that when a person becomes born again, the body of that individual now becomes the body of Jesus Christ. That is the reason why we must possess our bodies in true holiness. We cannot afford to do anything ungodly with the body of Christ. Read the passage of scripture from **Ephesians chapter 5** below.

Wives, submit yourselves unto your own husbands, as unto the Lord. For the husband is the head of the wife, even as Christ is the head of the church: and he is the saviour of the body. Therefore as the church is subject unto Christ, so let the wives be to their own husbands in every thing.

Husbands, love your wives, even as Christ also loved the church, and gave himself for it; That he might sanctify and cleanse it with the washing of water by the word, That he might present it to himself a glorious church, not having spot, or wrinkle, or any such thing; but that it should be holy and without blemish. So ought men to love their wives as their own bodies. He that loveth his wife loveth himself.

For no man ever yet hated his own flesh; but nourisheth and cherisheth it, even as the Lord the church: *for we are members of his body, of his flesh, and of his bones.* **For this cause shall a man leave his father and mother, and shall be joined unto his wife, and they two shall be one flesh.**

This is a great mystery: but I speak concerning Christ and the church. Nevertheless let every one of you in particular so love his wife even as himself; and the wife see that she reverence her husband.

Ephesians 5:22-33

We are now members of Jesus' body, bone of His bone and flesh of His flesh; *"But he that is joined unto the Lord is one spirit" (1 Corinthians 6:17).* Holiness is therefore a necessity as a Christian. Think about this carefully. You cannot engage in sex before marriage, nor drugs, nor consumption of alcohol nor any other forms of immorality with the body of Christ. If you come to this realisation, that your body is now that of Christ, you will not want to sin with it.

Your body is also the temple of the Holy Spirit so you must glorify God in your body. You see, the church mentioned in the above passage of scripture we read from **Ephesians chapter 5** does not refer to physical buildings. It refers to us as Christians. The church is now the individual who is born again and the Holy Spirit makes His home in that individual. The Holy Spirit cannot dwell in uncleanliness. It is therefore our duty as believers to ensure that we keep our bodies clean for the Lord. If you are entangled in any form of bondage or sexual immorality, ask the Lord for help and be ready and willing to stop. God is able to help you get out of bondage and keep you from falling.

Read the scripture below. Meditate on it and allow the Holy Spirit to minister to you.

Know ye not that the unrighteous shall not inherit the kingdom of God? Be not deceived: neither fornicators, nor idolaters, nor adulterers, nor effeminate, nor abusers of themselves with mankind, Nor thieves, nor covetous, nor drunkards, nor revilers, nor extortioners, shall inherit the kingdom of God. And such were some of you: but ye are washed, but ye are sanctified, but ye are justified in the name of the Lord Jesus, and by the Spirit of our God.

All things are lawful unto me, but all things are not expedient: all things are lawful for me, but I will not be brought under the power of any. Meats for the belly, and the belly for meats: but God shall destroy both it and them. Now the body is not for fornication, but for the Lord; and the Lord for the body. And God hath both raised up the Lord, and will also raise up us by his own power.

Know ye not that your bodies are the members of Christ? shall I then take the members of Christ, and make them the members

of an harlot? God forbid. What? know ye not that he which is joined to an harlot is one body? for two, saith he, shall be one flesh. But he that is joined unto the Lord is one spirit.

Flee fornication. Every sin that a man doeth is without the body; but he that committeth fornication sinneth against his own body. What? know ye not that your body is the temple of the Holy Ghost which is in you, which ye have of God, and ye are not your own? For ye are bought with a price: therefore glorify God in your body, and in your spirit, which are God's.

1 Corinthians 6:9-20

Wherefore come out from among them, and be ye separate, saith the Lord, and touch not the unclean thing; and I will receive you.

2 Corinthians 6:17

Chapter 6

Separation from the World

The moment you become a Christian, you must learn to separate yourself from the things you used to do in the world. If you keep on moving with the same friends, you will go back into the world. That it is why the Lord wants us to come out from among them and separate ourselves.

If you are now a believer, why are you still keeping that boyfriend or that girlfriend you used to have in the world? Can you not see that he or she is taking you backwards and pushing you further away from God? Cut off all such negative influences and be holy. I made a U-turn when I became born again and now the only friends I have are Christian friends who give me good counsel.

Be ye not unequally yoked together with unbelievers: for what fellowship hath righteousness with unrighteousness? and what communion hath light with darkness? And what concord hath Christ with Belial? or what part hath he that believeth with an infidel?

And what agreement hath the temple of God with idols? for ye are the temple of the living God; as God hath said, I will dwell

in them, and walk in them; and I will be their God, and they shall be my people. *wherefore come out from among them, and be ye separate*, **saith the Lord, and touch not the unclean thing; and I will receive you, and will be a father unto you, and ye shall be my sons and daughters, saith the Lord Almighty.**

2 Corinthians 6:14-18

Flee Sin.

For sin shall not have dominion over you: for ye are not under the law, but under grace.

Romans 6:14

And that ye put on the new man, which after God is created in righteousness and true holiness. Wherefore putting away lying, speak every man truth with his neighbour: for we are members one of another.

Ephesians 4:24-25

A Christian who continues to live in sin will never see the blessings of God. *Put on the new man* as the scripture says. Live the Christian life and cause your light to shine in this world.

Let your light so shine before men, that they may see your good works, and glorify your Father which is in heaven.

Matthew 5:16

Let people see the character of Jesus in you. Stop lying and fornicating and flee totally from sin. Sin shall not have dominion over you!

Righteousness exalteth a nation: but sin is a reproach to any people.

Proverbs 14:34

A Christian who lives a truly righteous and holy life will see God at work in their life and will be transformed from glory to glory. Such a Christian will be successful in everything that pertains to them. The word of God says that without holiness, no man shall see the Lord. This is very serious.

Follow peace with all men, and holiness, without which no man shall see the Lord.

Hebrews 12:14

The Christian life is a race and you cannot run forward with sin. You must lay aside every sin at the foot of the cross to enable you to finish the race. Athletes never have weights attached to their legs. As a matter of fact, they try to be as light as possible. They wear very light clothes to the point of exposing themselves. This is to cut off every weight that will impede how fast they run. It is the same with a Christian. How fast you run is determined by getting rid of sin from your life.

Wherefore seeing we also are compassed about with so great a cloud of witnesses, let us lay aside every weight, and the sin which doth so easily beset us, and let us run with patience the race that is set before us, Looking unto Jesus the author and finisher of our faith; who for the joy that was set before him endured the cross, despising the shame, and is set down at the right hand of the throne of God.

Hebrews 12:1-2

As newborn babes, desire the sincere milk of the word, that ye may grow thereby.

1 Peter 2:2

Chapter 7

Building the Spirit of Man

Now we know that the spirit is the most important dimension of man. So how do we develop it? Students go to school for years to develop their minds and body builders exercise continuously to develop their muscles. But the spirit of man does not grow by lifting weights or attending lectures. It grows by eating the word of God.

As newborn babes, desire the sincere milk of the word, that ye may grow thereby.

1 Peter 2:2

Once you are born again, the number one way to build your spirit is through the word of God. The following steps are good spiritual habits to help build up your spirit.

Read and meditate on the word of God daily.

The word of God is of paramount importance in our walk with the Lord. As a Christian, your entire life must be governed by the word of God. However, the word cannot direct and lead you until you have built up the inner man with the precious word of God.

1 Peter 2:2 tells us that we must *desire* the word, long for the word, eat the word of God so that we may grow. The physical body grows by eating physical food but food for the spirit is the word of God. Many churches are filled with baby Christians because they have not been built up with the word of God.

Spiritual growth only comes through the word. Feeding on the word of God will bring maturity to the body of Christ. It will transform us from baby Christians to mature Christians.

For when for the time ye ought to be teachers, ye have need that one teach you again which be the first principles of the oracles of God; and are become such as have need of milk, and not of strong meat.

For every one that useth milk is unskilful in the word of righteousness: for he is a babe. But strong meat belongeth to them that are of full age, even those who by reason of use have their senses exercised to discern both good and evil.

Hebrews 5:12-14

Read the word of God every day. As you read, pause and mediate on the word of God. To "meditate" means to *think through*. Think through a particular verse over and over again. The Lord commanded Joshua to do just that. Many blessings will come to you as you meditate on His word.

This book of the law shall not depart out of thy mouth; but thou shalt meditate therein day and night, that thou mayest observe to do according to all that is written therein: for then

thou shalt make thy way prosperous, and then thou shalt have good success.

Joshua 1:8

Blessed is the man that walketh not in the counsel of the ungodly, nor standeth in the way of sinners, nor sitteth in the seat of the scornful.

But his delight is in the law of the LORD; and in his law doth he meditate day and night.

And he shall be like a tree planted by the rivers of water, that bringeth forth his fruit in his season; his leaf also shall not wither; and whatsoever he doeth shall prosper.

Psalm 1:1-3

And it shall be, when he sitteth upon the throne of his kingdom, that he shall write him a copy of this law in a book out of that which is before the priests the Levites:

And it shall be with him, and he shall read therein all the days of his life: that he may learn to fear the LORD his God, to keep all the words of this law and these statutes, to do them.

Deuteronomy 17:18-19

Study the word of God at least once a week.

Reading and meditating on the word alone is not enough. We must go deeper and study the word of God.

Study to shew thyself approved unto God, a workman that needeth not to be ashamed, rightly dividing the word of truth.
2 Timothy 2:15

Studying is part of meditation because it allows you to pause and think about what you are reading. The word of God was written in Hebrew and Greek. You can use Greek and Hebrew dictionaries to check the original meanings of the words to give you more insight. This will help you to understand the word of God better. You can choose to study the bible on topics such as love, faith, the blood, the resurrection, the Holy Spirit or the lives of bible characters like Abraham or David.

Believe and trust in the word of God.

Trust in the LORD with all thine heart; and lean not unto thine own understanding. In all thy ways acknowledge him, and he shall direct thy paths. Be not wise in thine own eyes: fear the LORD, and depart from evil.
Proverbs 3:5-7

As a believer, you cannot trust in any other source of help apart from God. You cannot even trust in yourself and your own understanding. This is because when Adam and Eve fell, their minds also fell. The bible says that God gave them a reprobate mind which means a worthless mind to do all kinds of evil. This is why you cannot follow your own ways but only trust the word of God.

There is a way which seemeth right unto a man, but the end thereof are the ways of death.
Proverbs 14:12

The ways of man can only lead him to death and destruction because naturally, he is programmed to choose his own way and in doing so will go the wrong way. The Lord reminds us that His ways are not our ways and his thoughts are not our thoughts.

For my thoughts are not your thoughts, neither are your ways my ways, saith the LORD. For as the heavens are higher than the earth, so are my ways higher than your ways, and my thoughts than your thoughts.

Isaiah 55:8-9

Your life must be controlled by the word of God.

We must make a conscious effort to constantly apply the word of God in our lives daily. We must live the word and do it.

But be ye doers of the word, and not hearers only, deceiving your own selves.

James 1:22

And hereby we do know that we know him, if we keep his commandments.

1 John 2:3

My son, attend to my words; incline thine ear unto my sayings. Let them not depart from thine eyes; keep them in the midst of thine heart. For they are life unto those that find them, and health to all their flesh.

Proverbs 4:20-22

We will not benefit from the word if we do not apply it to our lives and practise it. If we live by the word, we will not steal, we will not hate and we will love our neighbours. The psalmist said that the entrance of God's word gives light and understanding to the simple *(Psalm 119:130)*. As you read the word, light comes into every area of your life and upon your very existence on earth. Suddenly you begin to have a sense of direction and purpose.

Use the word of God in decision making and put God first.

We must use the word of God in all decisions we take for in His word there is life. His word will make you rich and it will add no sorrow. I had to use the word of God to choose whom to marry. The bible says that Christians must not be unequally yoked with unbelievers. It is a direct command. A Christian cannot marry an unbeliever no matter how pretty or handsome they may look.

I have often rejected jobs that involved working on Sundays because I am commanded by the Lord to be in His house to worship Him. I remember a particular job interview where the interview panel were ready to give me the job. The employers actually said I was the right person for the job but with the condition that I must work one Sunday every month. I remember thinking about **Hebrews 10:25** which tells us not to forsake the assembling of the saints and I rejected that job. Shortly after making that decision, the Lord gave me a job that was only Monday to Friday. Hallelujah!

The Lord commanded the people of Israel to keep the word in their frontlets which meant that His word must always be their guide. Let the word of God be your guide in all areas today and everyday!

And these words, which I command thee this day, shall be in thine heart: And thou shalt teach them diligently unto thy children, and shalt talk of them when thou sittest in thine house, and when thou walkest by the way, and when thou liest down, and when thou risest up.

And thou shalt bind them for a sign upon thine hand, and they shall be as frontlets between thine eyes. And thou shalt write them upon the posts of thy house, and on thy gates.

Deuteronomy 6:6-9

Therefore shall ye lay up these my words in your heart and in your soul, and bind them for a sign upon your hand, that they may be as frontlets between your eyes.

And ye shall teach them your children, speaking of them when thou sittest in thine house, and when thou walkest by the way, when thou liest down, and when thou risest up.

And thou shalt write them upon the door posts of thine house, and upon thy gates: That your days may be multiplied, and the days of your children, in the land which the LORD sware unto your fathers to give them, as the days of heaven upon the earth.

Deuteronomy 11:18-21

Learn to listen to the promptings of the Holy Spirit through your spirit.

The Lord uses the spirit of man to guide him whether a person is born again or not. However, when a person is born again, their spirit becomes alive to God and so God can guide him closely and help him in taking vital decisions.

The spirit of man is the candle of the LORD, searching all the inward parts of the belly.

Proverbs 20:27

But there is a spirit in man: and the inspiration of the Almighty giveth them understanding.

Job 32:8

For what man knoweth the things of a man, save the spirit of man which is in him? even so the things of God knoweth no man, but the Spirit of God.

1 Corinthians 2:11

The Spirit itself beareth witness with our spirit, that we are the children of God.

Romans 8:16

All of the above verses of scriptures show how important our spirit is. We must learn to pay particular attention to our spirit. The spirit of man has a still small voice and it speaks from the inside. To "witness" means to *speak* and the Holy Spirit speaks to our spirit that which we are supposed to know.

I encourage you to develop these spiritual habits! Your spirit will be built up, your understanding of God's word will grow and the light of the word will shine on all areas of your life.

And they were all filled with the Holy Ghost, and began to speak with other tongues, as the Spirit gave them utterance.

Acts 2:4

Chapter 8

Praying in the Spirit

There is a lot of confusion in the body of Christ about praying in the Spirit or the more common expression, speaking in tongues. I think that this confusion is a result of misinterpretation of the holy word of God. Speaking in tongues is a language of the Holy Spirit that has been given as a promise to every believer. The Holy Spirit is the very Spirit of God and is also known as the Holy Ghost. I want to state that the Holy Spirit is **not** tongues but tongues are one of the many gifts of the Holy Spirit.

And they were all filled with the Holy Ghost, and began to speak with other tongues, as the Spirit gave them utterance.

Acts 2:4

And they of the circumcision which believed were astonished, as many as came with Peter, because that on the Gentiles also was poured out the gift of the Holy Ghost.

For they heard them speak with tongues, and magnify God. Then answered Peter, Can any man forbid water, that these should not be baptized, which have received the Holy Ghost as well as we?

Acts 10:45-47

And when Paul had laid his hands upon them, the Holy Ghost came on them; and they spake with tongues, and prophesied.

Acts 19:6

For with stammering lips and another tongue will he speak to this people.

Isaiah 28:11

And these signs shall follow them that believe; In my name shall they cast out devils; they shall speak with new tongues.

Mark 16:17

Then Peter said unto them, Repent, and be baptized every one of you in the name of Jesus Christ for the remission of sins, and ye shall receive the gift of the Holy Ghost.

For the promise is unto you, and to your children, and to all that are afar off, even as many as the Lord our God shall call.

Acts 2:38-39

In **Luke 24:49** and **Acts 1:4-5**, the Lord Jesus commanded the disciples to wait for the promise of the Father. They were to wait on God until they were endued with power from on high. This promise was fulfilled in **Acts chapter 2**. The disciples were filled with the Holy Spirit and the initial sign was speaking in tongues as they were enabled or *given utterance* by the Holy Spirit. Every believer must therefore desire to receive the gift of speaking in tongues. It is one of the greatest weapons that terrifies the kingdom of the enemy.

And, behold, I send the promise of my Father upon you: but tarry ye in the city of Jerusalem, until ye be endued with power from on high.

Luke 24:49

And, being assembled together with them, commanded them that they should not depart from Jerusalem, but wait for the promise of the Father, which, saith he, ye have heard of me. For John truly baptized with water; but ye shall be baptized with the Holy Ghost not many days hence.

Acts 1:4-5

Some churches deny speaking in tongues and say that speaking in tongues is of the devil. To say that speaking in tongues is of the devil is a blasphemy against the Holy Spirit and the bible declares that blasphemy against the Holy Ghost is a sin which shall never be forgiven.

Wherefore I say unto you, All manner of sin and blasphemy shall be forgiven unto men: but the blasphemy against the Holy Ghost shall not be forgiven unto men.

Matthew 12:31

I have also heard believers say that you can only speak in tongues when someone is present to interpret. This also is a misinterpretation of the word of God. The bible does not say so. The bible declares that you can speak in tongues whether someone is there to interpret it or not. Let us look at this area in **1 Corinthians 14:19** and **1 Corinthians 14:28**.

Yet in the church I had rather speak five words with my understanding, that by my voice I might teach others also, than ten thousand words in an unknown tongue.

1 Corinthians 14:19

But if there be no interpreter, let him keep silence in the church; and let him speak to himself, and to God.

1 Corinthians 14:28

1 Corinthians 14:19 clearly tells us that Paul was saying he cannot *preach* in tongues to the people. It does not mean that tongues cannot be spoken in the church. Neither does it mean that you cannot speak in tongues in the church unless there is an interpreter.

If you preach in tongues, certainly the church cannot understand, unless someone is there to interpret so as to edify the church. **1 Corinthians 14:28** reveals that you can speak in tongues to yourself in the church. However if you rise up to speak in tongues in the church when everyone is quiet, then there must be an interpretation so everyone in the congregation can understand what the Lord is telling His people.

When tongues are interpreted, it becomes a prophecy and it should exhort, comfort and edify the entire congregation.

But he that prophesieth speaketh unto men to edification, and exhortation, and comfort.

1 Corinthians 14:3

So the bible proves that you can speak in tongues both privately and publicly. But when speaking publicly, there must be an interpretation of whatsoever is being spoken.

Likewise the Spirit also helpeth our infirmities: for we know not what we should pray for as we ought: but the Spirit itself maketh intercession for us with groanings which cannot be uttered.

Romans 8:26

Chapter 9

Benefits of Speaking in Tongues for the Believer

There are many benefits of speaking in tongues apart from prophecy and as a weapon against the enemy. I will share just a few of these benefits with you.

You are able to pray in a language that no man understands.

For he that speaketh in an unknown tongue speaketh not unto men, but unto God: for no man understandeth him; howbeit in the spirit he speaketh mysteries.

1 Corinthians 14:2

You edify yourself as you pray in tongues.

He that speaketh in an unknown tongue edifieth himself; but he that prophesieth edifieth the church.

1 Corinthians 14:4

It increases your faith and builds you up spiritually.

But ye, beloved, building up yourselves on your most holy faith, praying in the Holy Ghost.

<div align="right">Jude 1:20</div>

You pray according to the will of God.

Likewise the Spirit also helpeth our infirmities: for we know not what we should pray for as we ought: but the Spirit itself maketh intercession for us with groanings which cannot be uttered.

And he that searcheth the hearts knoweth what is the mind of the Spirit, because he maketh intercession for the saints according to the will of God.

<div align="right">Romans 8:26-27</div>

Your spirit prays as the Holy Spirit gives your spirit utterance.

For if I pray in an unknown tongue, my spirit prayeth, but my understanding is unfruitful.

<div align="right">1 Corinthians 14:14</div>

You can give thanks to God well.

For thou verily givest thanks well, but the other is not edified.

<div align="right">1 Corinthians 14:17</div>

No wonder Apostle Paul who wrote more than half of the New Testament said in **1 Corinthians 14:18**, *"I thank my God, I speak with tongues more than ye all"*. When you think of all of these benefits, it is shocking to see believers rejecting such a valuable gift!

I love them that love me; and those that seek me early shall find me.

Proverbs 8:17

Chapter 10

Spend Time Alone with God

Spending time with the Lord is a good Christian habit. I am not talking about family devotion or group bible study or church service. I am talking about you as an individual Christian spending time with God. As an individual, you must learn how to spend time with your Creator and develop a relationship with Him. Two people who spend time together and talk to each other all the time are likely to bond and form a relationship.

As you spend time with the Lord in prayer, in reading His word, in worshipping Him then you will have a strong relationship with the Lord and you will begin to hear His precious voice. Choose a time in the day where you spend quality time with the Lord. The time should preferably be early in the morning.

I love them that love me; and those that seek me early shall find me.

Proverbs 8:17

Six ways you can spend time with the Lord

Here are just six ways you can spend time with the Lord.

Spend time daily in reading the word of God.

This book of the law shall not depart out of thy mouth; but thou shalt meditate therein day and night, that thou mayest observe to do according to all that is written therein: for then thou shalt make thy way prosperous, and then thou shalt have good success.

Joshua 1:8

Have a separate time where you study the word at least once a week.

Study to shew thyself approved unto God, a workman that needeth not to be ashamed, rightly dividing the word of truth.

2 Timothy 2:15

Memorise Scriptures.

My people are destroyed for lack of knowledge: because thou hast rejected knowledge, I will also reject thee, that thou shalt be no priest to me: seeing thou hast forgotten the law of thy God, I will also forget thy children.

Hosea 4:6

Write or type single verses on cards and memorise them. You
memorise **John 3:16, Matthew 6:33** and many other wonderful

scriptures. David said that *"thy word have I hid in mine heart, that I might not sin against thee" (Psalm 119:11).*

Read Christian books written by anointed preachers of God.

Spend money to buy anointed Christian books and read them. This is another way of getting the word of God into your spirit to grow. Avoid spending time reading unnecessary things. Stop reading books from unbelievers who are into all kinds of witchcraft activities. As you read their dead books, you receive what is upon them. Speak to the Lord to lead you to buy and read anointed Christian books.

And I went unto the angel, and said unto him, Give me the little book. And he said unto me, Take it, and eat it up; and it shall make thy belly bitter, but it shall be in thy mouth sweet as honey. And I took the little book out of the angel's hand, and ate it up; and it was in my mouth sweet as honey: and as soon as I had eaten it, my belly was bitter. And he said unto me, Thou must prophesy again before many peoples, and nations, and tongues, and kings.

Revelation 10:9-11

Moreover he said unto me, Son of man, eat that thou findest; eat this roll, and go speak unto the house of Israel. So I opened my mouth, and he caused me to eat that roll.

And he said unto me, Son of man, cause thy belly to eat, and fill thy bowels with this roll that I give thee.

Then did I eat it; and it was in my mouth as honey for sweetness.

And he said unto me, Son of man, go, get thee unto the house of Israel, and speak with my words unto them.

Ezekiel 3:1-4

Spend time in prayer and worship.

You can combine reading of the word with prayer during this time. Spend at least 15 minutes reading the bible and 15 minutes in prayer every morning before leaving your house. As you continue steadfastly, the time will increase and increase and you would not like to miss even a day of spending time with the Lord.

My voice shalt thou hear in the morning, O LORD; in the morning will I direct my prayer unto thee, and will look up.

Psalm 5:3

Learn to go away on retreats where you spend time with the Lord in prayer, in worship and in reading and studying of the word.

Aside from your daily time with the Lord every morning, have a place far from your house where you go and meet the Lord. Turn off your mobile phones and any communication systems and just be with the Lord. Jesus is our best example.

And it came to pass in those days, that he went out into a mountain to pray, and continued all night in prayer to God.

Luke 6:12

Listen to preaching messages, gospel music and watch preaching videos.

Instead of listening to radio and watching unnecessary television programmes for endless hours, you should rather spend time listening to preaching messages and watching preaching videos. I call the television a one-eye monster. It is a monster because it has snatched most believers from the presence of God. It is a demon in disguise and many believers have fallen for it. Christians watch television throughout Saturday night and miss Sunday service. They watch demonic movies and images on the television all the time.

If you can only switch the time you spend watching television and listening to radio to watching and listening to preaching messages, it will change your life for good. Jesus told the disciples that *"the words that I speak to you they are spirit and they are life"* in *(John 6:63)*. Spend money and buy preaching videos and preaching messages. Invest in these materials and you will be blessed.

It is the spirit that quickeneth; the flesh profiteth nothing: the words that I speak unto you, they are spirit, and they are life.
John 6:63

The power of God can reach you and fall on you while watching or listening to a preaching message. The words are *spirit* and *life* and can permeate your very being while watching and listening. Many believers have received their breakthrough, deliverance and anointing while listening to preaching messages and videos.

And the spirit entered into me when he spake unto me, and set me upon my feet, that I heard him that spake unto me.

Ezekiel 2:2

While Peter yet spake these words, the Holy Ghost fell on all them which heard the word.

Acts 10:44

Now, Jesus described the devil as the prince of the power of the air. Satan has taken charge over the atmosphere through music. He himself was a worshiper and therefore through the power of music, he has been able to infiltrate many lives. The youth of today have their minds captured by worldly music and their lives have become the strongholds of demons.

Wherein in time past ye walked according to the course of this world, according to the prince of the power of the air, the spirit that now worketh in the children of disobedience.

Ephesians 2:2

Avoid listening to worldly songs and fill your life with anointed Christian praise and worship songs. Before I became a believer, I listened to songs by people who were not Christians. After reading the word of God in **John 6:63**, I destroyed all those CDs and I never returned to them. I have stopped listening to worldly songs.

You see, when you listen to these songs, the demon and the spirit of the one you are listening to comes on you just like the Holy Ghost fell on the people whilst they were listening to Peter in **Acts 10**. Worldly music is one of the surest ways by which demons enter into people's lives and homes.

I often advise church members to play worship songs and preaching messages in their homes and cars to drive out demons and create an atmosphere where God lives. Delete all the demonic songs from your phone, your computer and your iPod and start listening to Christian songs.

Not forsaking the assembling of ourselves together, as the manner of some is; but exhorting one another: and so much the more, as ye see the day approaching.

Hebrews 10:25

Chapter 11

Regular Fellowship

Earlier I mentioned that our minds must be renewed about going to church. The Lord commands us to go to church because He expects His people to gather together in fellowship. People have developed all kinds of ideologies about going to church in order to ignore this basic Christian truth. Many born again Christians do not go to church for trivial reasons. I have heard people give reasons ranging from being offended, disliking the pastor, to too much offerings being taken. All of these are poor excuses to justify not attending church.

Not forsaking the assembling of ourselves together, as the manner of some is; but exhorting one another: and so much the more, as ye see the day approaching.

Hebrews 10:25

As born again Christians we must lay such reasons aside. We need to understand that it is a commandment from the Lord for all believers to go to church. People attend church with different needs and different intentions. Generally speaking, once those needs and intentions are satisfied, shallow believers will leave their church and stop fellowshipping. But by doing so, they have completely missed the reason why we go to church. Christians should not go to church because of the pastor, or a friend, or a partner but because of the Lord Jesus Christ. We go to church to worship and serve our God. We go to church to get to know Him better. We go to receive His word that is able to save our souls. Hallelujah!

Some Christians say they would rather stay at home and worship God but this is a great deception that the devil is throwing in the eyes of believers. **Hebrews 10:25**, instructs us not to isolate ourselves from the gathering of the saints. It reminds us that we should encourage one another to attend church.

I sometimes watch documentaries on the animal kingdom and in doing so, I have observed a common trick of the enemy. For example, you will see that whenever a deer singles itself from its group, it becomes an easy target and often ends up as meat for the lion. But when the deer are in a group, it becomes very difficult for the lions to attack them. A Christian who does not attend church often will deteriorate and degenerate into an unbeliever.

If you separate a coal of fire from the whole fire, that single coal of fire will eventually die out. It is the same with an isolated Christian; their fire will die with time. So you see it is very dangerous to joke with attending church. Christians who separate themselves from going to church are not spiritually strong because if they were, they will see that the devil is separating them to sift them like wheat. The word of God states that those who separate themselves have not the Holy Spirit.

These be they who separate themselves, sensual, having not the Spirit.

Jude 1:19

When the Lord appeared to the disciples after His resurrection, Thomas was absent and therefore he did not believe that Christ has truly risen. This is what happens to most believers. As you stay away from fellowship with other believers, you begin to doubt and drift from the Lord.

Thomas, one of the twelve disciples was used to separating himself and he was the one who lacked faith the most. His Christian life was affected and he began to doubt the very words Jesus spoke to the disciples before His death.

Then the same day at evening, being the first day of the week, when the doors were shut where the disciples were assembled for fear of the Jews, came Jesus and stood in the midst, and saith unto them, Peace be unto you. And when he had so said, he shewed unto them his hands and his side. Then were the disciples glad, when they saw the Lord. Then said Jesus to them again, Peace be unto you: as my Father hath sent me, even so send I you. And when he had said this, he breathed on them, and saith unto them, Receive ye the Holy Ghost: Whose soever sins ye remit, they are remitted unto them; and whose soever sins ye retain, they are retained.

But Thomas, one of the twelve, called Didymus, was not with them when Jesus came. The other disciples therefore said unto him, We have seen the Lord. But he said unto them, Except I shall see in his hands the print of the nails, and put my finger into the print of the nails, and thrust my hand into his side, I will not believe.

And after eight days again his disciples were within, and Thomas with them: then came Jesus, the doors being shut, and stood in the midst, and said, Peace be unto you. Then saith he to Thomas, Reach hither thy finger, and behold my hands; and reach hither thy hand, and thrust it into my side: and be not faithless, but believing. And Thomas answered and said unto him, My Lord and my God. Jesus saith unto him, Thomas, because thou hast seen me, thou hast believed: blessed are they that have not seen, and yet have believed.

John 20:19-29

The secret of having regular fellowship with other believers and going to church is that the Lord Jesus is always present where His people are gathered. It is good to spend time with God alone but that is different from going to church. It is wrong to stay at home and watch another church on the television when you know that you have to go to church. The people you are watching on the television are in church but you are not!

Jesus always visits His church and the disciples learnt that key. I often advise Christians to find a good bible believing church where the solid word of God is taught to attend. Carefully read the following scriptures about fellowship and do likewise.

Again I say unto you, That if two of you shall agree on earth as touching any thing that they shall ask, it shall be done for them of my Father which is in heaven.

For where two or three are gathered together in my name, there am I in the midst of them.

Matthew 18:19-20

And when the day of Pentecost was fully come, *they were all with one accord in one place*. And suddenly there came a sound from heaven as of a rushing mighty wind, and it filled all the house where they were sitting.

And there appeared unto them cloven tongues like as of fire, and it sat upon each of them. And *they were all filled* with the Holy Ghost, and began to speak with other tongues, as the Spirit gave them utterance.

Acts 2:1-4

And they continued stedfastly in the apostles' doctrine and fellowship, and in breaking of bread, and in prayers.

Acts 2:42

And when they were come in, they went up into an upper room, where abode both Peter, and James, and John, and Andrew, Philip, and Thomas, Bartholomew, and Matthew, James the son of Alphaeus, and Simon Zelotes, and Judas the brother of James.

These all continued with one accord in prayer and supplication, with the women, and Mary the mother of Jesus, and with his brethren.

Acts 1:13-14

And he said unto them, Go ye into all the world, and preach the gospel to every creature.

Mark 16:15

Chapter 12

Daily Witnessing

Every believer is called of God to bring others to Christ. This is a great duty of all Christians whether they are pastors or not. It is the greatest commandment that God gave to his church to go into all the world and make disciples.

Without this, many will head to hell and their blood will be required of us. We must bring our friends, families, work colleagues and anyone we meet on the street to Jesus. It is our duty to testify about Jesus Christ.

The Lord has called every believer to bear fruits in His kingdom and our fruits are souls.

Ye have not chosen me, but I have chosen you, and ordained you, that ye should go and bring forth fruit, and that your fruit should remain: that whatsoever ye shall ask of the Father in my name, he may give it you.

John 15:16

The Lord has commanded every believer to go into the world and preach the gospel to every person.

And he said unto them, Go ye into all the world, and preach the gospel to every creature.

Mark 16:15

Go ye therefore, and teach all nations, baptizing them in the name of the Father, and of the Son, and of the Holy Ghost:

Teaching them to observe all things whatsoever I have commanded you: and, lo, I am with you alway, even unto the end of the world. Amen.

Matthew 28:19-20

The blood of the wicked will be required of us if we fail to tell them about Jesus.

When I say unto the wicked, Thou shalt surely die; and thou givest him not warning, nor speakest to warn the wicked from his wicked way, to save his life; the same wicked man shall die in his iniquity; but his blood will I require at thine hand. Yet if thou warn the wicked, and he turn not from his wickedness, nor from his wicked way, he shall die in his iniquity; but thou hast delivered thy soul.

Again, When a righteous man doth turn from his righteousness, and commit iniquity, and I lay a stumbling-block before him, he shall die: because thou hast not given him warning, he shall die in his sin, and his righteousness which he hath done shall not be remembered; but his blood will I require at thine hand.

Nevertheless if thou warn the righteous man, that the righteous sin not, and he doth not sin, he shall surely live, because he is warned; also thou hast delivered thy soul.

Ezekiel 3:18-21

But this I say, He which soweth sparingly shall reap also sparingly; and he which soweth bountifully shall reap also bountifully.

2 Corinthians 9:6

Chapter 13

Giving to Support the Kingdom of God

In the world, we are taught to receive but in the kingdom of God, you sow first and then you reap. Every believer must learn to give offerings and pay tithes in their churches. Do not allow offerings and tithes to take you out of the church. Do you love money more than God? God gives you the power to make wealth.

But this I say, He which soweth sparingly shall reap also sparingly; and he which soweth bountifully shall reap also bountifully.

2 Corinthians 9:6

Be not deceived; God is not mocked: for whatsoever a man soweth, that shall he also reap.

Galatians 6:7

But thou shalt remember the LORD thy God: for it is he that giveth thee power to get wealth, that he may establish his covenant which he sware unto thy fathers, as it is this day.

Deuteronomy 8:18

Christians sometimes behave like babies when it comes to giving to support God's work. Imagine if a parent gives their child food and then says 'give me some of the food' and the child refuses. This is how most Christians behave about financial giving in the kingdom of God and it is wrong in the sight of God. Whether you give or not, it does not affect God. We should give because we love God and we want to support His work for more souls to be won.

Jesus tells us in **Acts 20:35** that it is more blessed to give than to receive. We must therefore give to expand the work of God and to win more souls into the kingdom of God. It is true that many pastors have turned into vampires sucking the blood of the church. I promise you that God has honest and faithful pastors who will not spend the money that belongs to the church but will use the money to further expand the gospel.

It is one of your Christian obligations to the Lord to give to support His kingdom. We can start more churches and send out more missionaries if every believer realises why we give offerings and pay tithes. We must give to build more church buildings. If every believer will understand that ten percent of all their earnings belong to the Lord, the kingdom of God will expand greatly.

There are several ways you can support the kingdom of God to expand. Primarily, you can do so through your offerings and tithes but there are other ways of also supporting God's work.

Offerings

The children of Israel brought a willing offering unto the LORD, every man and woman, whose heart made them

willing to bring for all manner of work, which the LORD had commanded to be made by the hand of Moses.

Exodus 35:29

Tithing

Will a man rob God? Yet ye have robbed me. But ye say, Wherein have we robbed thee? In tithes and offerings. Ye are cursed with a curse: for ye have robbed me, even this whole nation.

Bring ye all the tithes into the storehouse, that there may be meat in mine house, and prove me now herewith, saith the LORD of hosts, if I will not open you the windows of heaven, and pour you out a blessing, that there shall not be room enough to receive it.

And I will rebuke the devourer for your sakes, and he shall not destroy the fruits of your ground; neither shall your vine cast her fruit before the time in the field, saith the LORD of hosts. And all nations shall call you blessed: for ye shall be a delightsome land, saith the LORD of hosts.

Malachi 3:8-12

For this God is our God for ever and ever:
he will be our guide even unto death.

Psalm 48:14

Chapter 14

Total Commitment to God

Almighty God is totally committed to us. Read the scriptures below carefully and ask the Holy Spirit to help you to understand the deepest meaning of these scriptures.

For this God is our God for ever and ever: he will be our guide even unto death.

Psalm 48:14

For ever, O LORD, thy word is settled in heaven.

Psalm 119:89

My covenant will I not break, nor alter the thing that is gone out of my lips.

Psalm 89:34

Then said the LORD unto me, Thou hast well seen: for I will hasten my word to perform it.

Jeremiah 1:12

God is not a man, that he should lie; neither the son of man, that he should repent: hath he said, and shall he not do it? or hath he spoken, and shall he not make it good?

Numbers 23:19

That by two immutable things, in which it was impossible for God to lie, we might have a strong consolation, who have fled for refuge to lay hold upon the hope set before us.

Hebrews 6:18

Let your conversation be without covetousness; and be content with such things as ye have: for he hath said, I will never leave thee, nor forsake thee.

Hebrews 13:5

When you receive salvation and become born again, you become a child of God.

But as many as received him, to them gave he power to become the sons of God, even to them that believe on his name.

John 1:12

You are now His child so God becomes totally committed to you and to your life, to bring you to the expected end by ensuring that His plans for your life comes to pass at all cost.

For I know the thoughts that I think toward you, saith the LORD, thoughts of peace, and not of evil, to give you an expected end.

Jeremiah 29:11

God says in **Hebrews 13:5** that He will never leave us nor forsake us. His commitment and love for us is unconditional. It does not depend on whether we fail or not. Even when we fail Him and deny Him, He is still committed to us.

If we believe not, yet he abideth faithful: he cannot deny himself.
2 Timothy 2:13

God will still remain faithful to us, even if we do not believe in Him because He cannot deny His faithful nature. God never changes towards us. We as human beings change but God always remain the same.

Five ways to be committed to the Lord and His Work

As a born again believer, your duty is to have an unchanging commitment to the Lord and to His work. Be committed to the Lord in your daily fellowship to Him. Be committed to reading His word. But I tell you the truth, being committed to the Lord alone is not enough. He has also ordained you to do His work.

For we are his workmanship, created in Christ Jesus unto good works, which God hath before ordained that we should walk in them.
Ephesians 2:10

We are God's workmanship. As soon as we become born again, we become partners with God to do His work. He created this for us before we were even formed in our mother's womb. He actually chose us to bring forth fruit in His kingdom.

Ye have not chosen me, but I have chosen you, and ordained you, that ye should go and bring forth fruit, and that your fruit should remain: that whatsoever ye shall ask of the Father in my name, he may give it you.

John 15:16

So how can we show our commitment to the Lord? Here are five ways in which you can demonstrate your commitment to Him.

1. **Be committed to prayer.**

2. **Be committed to reading and studying the bible.**

3. **Be committed to winning souls.**

4. **Be involved in the work of your local church.**

By this I mean join in the regular church activities. Do not just be a church goer but do something in your local church! Join the choir, the ushers, the prayer team, the welcoming team or any such ministries in your church. It will help you to be committed to the Lord and to be fruitful in His house. Not being involved in any of the activities of your local church shows that you are not committed to the Lord. Go for prayer meetings and evangelistic programmes to win souls into the kingdom of God. Make your God-given talents available to God and to His church.

5. **Be committed to financially supporting your church by paying your tithes regularly and giving offerings.**

Be committed to seeking the Lord and getting to know Him all the days of your life. By doing so, you will not only demonstrate your love for God but you will also draw closer to Him. Now that you know who you are in Christ and how you should live as a Christian, I believe that your relationship with the Lord will be strengthened and will move to a deeper level.

The Lord is ready to have a closer relationship with you. He has been waiting for you for a long time. Being born again is just a step into divine glory that is prepared for you. Step into it as you deepen your relationship with your Creator! I see you being transformed as you develop your spirit, soul and body! I see you getting closer to God! I see you becoming a strong Christian! I see you being established in His kingdom! I see you being rooted and grounded in His love! I see you being blessed! I see you being lifted up! In the mighty name of Jesus Christ. AMEN.

Study to shew thyself approved unto God, a workman that needeth not to be ashamed, rightly dividing the word of truth.

2 Timothy 2:15

Chapter 15

Solid Foundation of the Word

The Bible tells us in **2 Timothy 3:16** that all scripture is written by the inspiration of God. Almighty God spoke through holy men of God to write down the scriptures. Therefore, God the Father, God the Son and God the Holy Spirit is the author of the scriptures.

A born again Christian cannot grow spiritually except through the Word of God. To grow properly as a Christian, you must eat biblical scriptures like food. The Holy Scriptures provide the spiritual food to build us up. Therefore, as a Christian, you must desire the sincere milk of the word of God so that you can develop well.

A Christian's life is like a house that is being built and it requires a solid foundation. A house without a good foundation will certainly collapse as the years pass and natural disasters take place. This is the reason why builders ensure that the foundation of a house is well-built to survive disasters. Your Christian life must have a solid foundation that remains unshakeable during the storms of life. Such a foundation can only be built upon the solid rock of the word of God. As Apostle Paul said, we must be *steadfast, unmoveable* and *always abounding* in the Lord *(1 Corinthians 15:58)*.

Therefore whosoever heareth these sayings of mine, and doeth them, I will liken him unto a wise man, which built his house upon a rock:

And the rain descended, and the floods came, and the winds blew, and beat upon that house; and it fell not: for it was founded upon a rock.

And every one that heareth these sayings of mine, and doeth them not, shall be likened unto a foolish man, which built his house upon the sand:

And the rain descended, and the floods came, and the winds blew, and beat upon that house; and it fell: and great was the fall of it.

Matthew 7:24-27

The above passage of scripture gives an illustration of two people who were both building their houses. One built the foundation of the house upon the sand and the other built upon the rock. When the torrents of rain, and floods and winds hit both houses vehemently, the house that was built upon the sand could not stand. It was completely destroyed. The house which was established upon the solid rock survived the storms of life.

These two houses can be likened to how two types of believers have chosen to build their Christian lives. The rock in the scripture symbolises the word of God and the sand represents the traditions of men. When you build your Christian life on the traditions of men and what people say you will not be able to stand. If you do not learn the scriptures for yourself to know whether those hearsays are true or not, you shall fall when the storms of life hit you. But a Christian, who has a firm foundation in the word of God, shall surely stand as the storms of life manifest. This is because the rock which is the word of God can never be destroyed. The word of God states that *"For ever, O LORD, thy word is settled in heaven" (Psalm 119:89).*

Reading and Studying the Word

Reading the word of God daily is vital as a Christian. Reading helps us to get general information. For instance you can read the bible and know the stories of the Prodigal Son, the Good Samaritan, Lazarus and the Rich Man, the stories of people like Moses, David and so forth. These stories all contain important information and provide valuable lessons for Christians. I always have a book in the bible that I am reading at any point in time.

However, reading is different from studying. You read to get information but you study to gain understanding and to apply the understanding to daily life. The word of God encourages us to study to show ourselves approved unto God.

These are more noble than those in Thessalonica in that they received the word in all readiness of mind, and searched the scriptures daily, whether those things were so.

Acts 17:11

The word "Search" in **Acts 17:11** is the Greek word "Anakrino" which means: *scrutinise, investigate, discern, examine* and *search.* These definitions makes it clear that a Christian should not just read ⁺ˡ word of God but must have time dedicated for searching, examining and studying the precious word of God.

In **2 Timothy 2:15**, the word "Study" is the Greek word "Spoudazo" which means to *labour*. We know that labour requires an ample amount of time. Studying therefore requires time. You cannot read the word of God for five minutes and call it studying. Studying just a verse in the bible can take you hours, days and even months but by all means do your best to study the word of God at least once a week.

When I was growing up as a Christian, I gave myself to studying God's word. My spiritual father emphasised the importance of having a solid foundation in the scriptures. I would write down scriptures given to me by my pastor on cards and literally memorise them. I even memorised the scriptures he used whilst preaching! It may interest you to know that I still listen to my spiritual father, Bishop Dag Heward-Mills. This has given me a very solid foundation.

Dedicate one day in the week where you study the word of God for a few hours. You will need some tools to help you study effectively.

Tools for studying the Bible

1. A good bible.

You need a good bible to study the word of God. A dry bible is like bread without butter. It is very difficult to swallow dry bread. Likewise, ve a plain bible without has no concordance and background on of scriptures, it will make studying very difficult. Invest in es with extended commentaries such as Thompson's Chain

Reference bible and Dakes Annotated Reference bible. These are very good for studying the bible. The Thompson's Chain Reference bible gives you a chain of scriptures referring to particular topics like faith, love, patience and so forth while the Dakes gives you both the Hebrew and Greek meaning of words. A person who wants to be a good student of the word of God must acquire a useful bible.

2. Greek and Hebrew Dictionaries.

The original languages of the bible are Greek and Hebrew. If you therefore want to really understand the true meaning of the words, you will need a Greek and Hebrew dictionary. I have often used Strongest Strong concordance which is a very good Greek and Hebrew dictionary for the bible.

3. A good English Dictionary.

There are several good English dictionaries out there but I will recommend Oxford dictionary as I have found it very useful in studying the word of God.

4. A Notebook.

This is a book where you write down your findings. With modern gadgets such as our mobile phones, iPads, tablets and so forth, it very easy to record your findings. Nonetheless, an ordinary notebook is still a useful tool. You can write your notes and you do not need electricity to turn it on nor will it run out of battery!

Below are scriptures that I memorised while growing up as a Christian. Give yourself to learning them by heart. You are reading this book as a result of the solid foundation of the scriptures at work in my life. I am imparting to you that which I have received and I know your entire life will never be the same as you give yourself to studying and memorising the Holy Scriptures.

All scriptures are taken from
King James Version of the Bible.

Exodus

And the blood shall be to you for a token upon the houses where ye are: and when I see the blood, I will pass over you, and the plague shall not be upon you to destroy you, when I smite the land of Egypt.
Exodus 12:13

And said, If thou wilt diligently hearken to the voice of the Lord thy God, and wilt do that which is right in his sight, and wilt give ear to his commandments, and keep all his statutes, I will put none of these diseases upon thee, which I have brought upon the Egyptians: for I am the Lord that healeth thee.
Exodus 15:26

And ye shall serve the Lord your God, and he shall bless thy bread, and thy water; and I will take sickness away from the midst of thee.

There shall nothing cast their young, nor be barren, in thy land: the number of thy days I will fulfil.
Exodus 23:25-26

Numbers

And the Lord said unto Moses, Gather unto me seventy men of the elders of Israel, whom thou knowest to be the elders of the people, and officers over them; and bring them unto the tabernacle of the congregation, that they may stand there with thee.

And I will come down and talk with thee there: and I will take of the spirit which is upon thee, and will put it upon them; and they shall bear the burden of the people with thee, that thou bear it not thyself alone.

Numbers 11:16-17

God is not a man, that he should lie; neither the son of man, that he should repent: hath he said, and shall he not do it? or hath he spoken, and shall he not make it good?

Numbers 23:19

Deuteronomy

But thou shalt remember the Lord thy God: for it is he that giveth thee power to get wealth, that he may establish his covenant which he sware unto thy fathers, as it is this day.

Deuteronomy 8:18

Joshua

This book of the law shall not depart out of thy mouth; but thou shalt meditate therein day and night, that thou mayest observe to do according to all that is written therein: for then thou shalt make thy way prosperous, and then thou shalt have good success.

Have not I commanded thee? Be strong and of a good courage; be not afraid, neither be thou dismayed: for the Lord thy God is with thee whithersoever thou goest.

Joshua 1:8-9

Now Joshua was old and stricken in years; and the Lord said unto him, Thou art old and stricken in years, and there remaineth yet very much land to be possessed.

Joshua 13:1

1 Samuel

And Samuel said, Hath the Lord as great delight in burnt offerings and sacrifices, as in obeying the voice of the Lord? Behold, to obey is better than sacrifice, and to hearken than the fat of rams.

For rebellion is as the sin of witchcraft, and stubbornness is as iniquity and idolatry. Because thou hast rejected the word of the Lord, he hath also rejected thee from being king.

1 Samuel 15:22-23

1 Samuel

But the Lord said unto Samuel, Look not on his countenance, or on the height of his stature; because I have refused him: for the Lord seeth not as man seeth; for man looketh on the outward appearance, but theLord looketh on the heart.

1 Samuel 16:7

2 Chronicles

If my people, which are called by my name, shall humble themselves, and pray, and seek my face, and turn from their wicked ways; then will I hear from heaven, and will forgive their sin, and will heal their land.

2 Chronicles 7:14

And they rose early in the morning, and went forth into the wilderness of Tekoa: and as they went forth, Jehoshaphat stood and said, Hear me, O Judah, and ye inhabitants of Jerusalem; Believe in the Lord your God, so shall ye be established; believe his prophets, so shall ye prosper.

2 Chronicles 20:20

Ezra

For Ezra had prepared his heart to seek the law of the Lord, and to do it, and to teach in Israel statutes and judgments.

Ezra 7:10

Nehemiah

Then answered I them, and said unto them, The God of heaven, he will prosper us; therefore we his servants will arise and build: but ye have no portion, nor right, nor memorial, in Jerusalem.

Nehemiah 2:20

Esther

For if thou altogether holdest thy peace at this time, then shall there enlargement and deliverance arise to the Jews from another place; but thou and thy father's house shall be destroyed: and who knoweth whether thou art come to the kingdom for such a time as this?

Esther 4:14

Job

And the Lord said unto Satan, Whence comest thou? Then Satan answered the Lord, and said, From going to and fro in the earth, and from walking up and down in it.

Job 1:7

Is there not an appointed time to man upon earth? are not his days also like the days of an hireling?

Job 7:1

Man that is born of a woman is of few days and full of trouble.

Job 14:1

Psalms

O taste and see that the Lord is good: blessed is the man that trusteth in him.

Psalm 34:8

The Lord will not leave him in his hand, nor condemn him when he is judged.

Psalm 37:33

A thousand shall fall at thy side, and ten thousand at thy right hand; but it shall not come nigh thee.

Psalm 91:7

Those that be planted in the house of the Lord shall flourish in the courts of our God.

Psalm 92:13

Psalms

Bless the Lord, O my soul: and all that is within me, bless his holy name.

Bless the Lord, O my soul, and forget not all his benefits:

Who forgiveth all thine iniquities; who healeth all thy diseases.

Psalm 103:1-3

Wherewithal shall a young man cleanse his way? by taking heed thereto according to thy word.

Psalm 119:9

I have more understanding than all my teachers: for thy testimonies are my meditation.

Psalm 119:99

Thy word is a lamp unto my feet, and a light unto my path.

Psalm 119:105

The entrance of thy words giveth light; it giveth understanding unto the simple.

Psalm 119:130

Many are my persecutors and mine enemies; yet do I not decline from thy testimonies.

Psalm 119:157

My soul hath kept thy testimonies; and I love them exceedingly.

Psalm 119:167

When the Lord turned again the captivity of Zion, we were like them that dream.

Then was our mouth filled with laughter, and our tongue with singing: then said they among the heathen, The Lord hath done great things for them.

Psalm 126:1-2

Except the Lord build the house, they labour in vain that build it: except the Lord keep the city, the watchman waketh but in vain.

Psalm 127:1

Lo, children are an heritage of the Lord: and the fruit of the womb is his reward.

Psalm 127:3

Behold, how good and how pleasant it is for brethren to dwell together in unity!

Psalm 133:1

Proverbs

Trust in the Lord with all thine heart; and lean not unto thine own understanding.

In all thy ways acknowledge him, and he shall direct thy paths.

Proverbs 3:5-6

My son, attend to my words; incline thine ear unto my sayings. Let them not depart from thine eyes; keep them in the midst of thine heart.

For they are life unto those that find them, and health to all their flesh.

Keep thy heart with all diligence; for out of it are the issues of life.

Proverbs 4:20-23

A false balance is abomination to the Lord: but a just weight is his delight.

Proverbs 11:1

The light of the righteous rejoiceth: but the lamp of the wicked shall be put out.

Only by pride cometh contention: but with the well advised is wisdom.

Proverbs 13:9-10

There is a way which seemeth right unto a man, but the end thereof are the ways of death.

Proverbs 14:12

A soft answer turneth away wrath: but grievous words stir up anger.

Proverbs 15:1

A good name is rather to be chosen than great riches, and loving favour rather than silver and gold.

Proverbs 22:1

Through wisdom is an house builded; and by understanding it is established:

And by knowledge shall the chambers be filled with all precious and pleasant riches.

Proverbs 24:3-4

Where there is no vision, the people perish: but he that keepeth the law, happy is he.

Proverbs 29:18

Ecclesiastes

The thing that hath been, it is that which shall be; and that which is done is that which shall be done: and there is no new thing under the sun.

Is there anything whereof it may be said, See, this is new? it hath been already of old time, which was before us.

Ecclesiastes 1:9-10

To every thing there is a season, and a time to every purpose under the heaven:

Ecclesiastes 3:1

He hath made every thing beautiful in his time: also he hath set the world in their heart, so that no man can find out the work that God maketh from the beginning to the end.

Ecclesiastes 3:11

There is one alone, and there is not a second; yea, he hath neither child nor brother: yet is there no end of all his labour; neither is his eye satisfied with riches; neither saith he, For whom do I labour, and bereave my soul of good? This is also vanity, yea, it is a sore travail.

Ecclesiastes 4:8

Two are better than one; because they have a good reward for their labour.

Ecclesiastes 4:9

When thou vowest a vow unto God, defer not to pay it; for he hath no pleasure in fools: pay that which thou hast vowed.

Ecclesiastes 5:4

Behold that which I have seen: it is good and comely for one to eat and to drink, and to enjoy the good of all his labour that he taketh under the sun all the days of his life, which God giveth him: for it is his portion.

Ecclesiastes 5:18

A good name is better than precious ointment; and the day of death than the day of one's birth.

Ecclesiastes 7:1

Live joyfully with the wife whom thou lovest all the days of the life of thy vanity, which he hath given thee under the sun, all the days of thy vanity: for that is thy portion in this life, and in thy labour which thou takest under the sun.

Ecclesiastes 9:9

Whatsoever thy hand findeth to do, do it with thy might; for there is no work, nor device, nor knowledge, nor wisdom, in the grave, whither thou goest.

Ecclesiastes 9:10

Ecclesiastes

There was a little city, and few men within it; and there came a great king against it, and besieged it, and built great bulwarks against it: Now there was found in it a poor wise man, and he by his wisdom delivered the city; yet no man remembered that same poor man. Then said I, Wisdom is better than strength: nevertheless the poor man's wisdom is despised, and his words are not heard.

Ecclesiastes 9:14-16

Woe to thee, O land, when thy king is a child, and thy princes eat in the morning! Blessed art thou, O land, when thy king is the son of nobles, and thy princes eat in due season, for strength, and not for drunkenness!

Ecclesiastes 10:16-17

Cast thy bread upon the waters: for thou shalt find it after many days.

Ecclesiastes 11:1

Remember now thy Creator in the days of thy youth, while the evil days come not, nor the years draw nigh, when thou shalt say, I have no pleasure in them;

Ecclesiastes 12:1

Let us hear the conclusion of the whole matter: Fear God, and keep his commandments: for this is the whole duty of man.

Ecclesiastes 12:13

Let us hear the conclusion of the whole matter: Fear God, and keep his commandments: for this is the whole duty of man.

Ecclesiastes 12:13

Isaiah

Come now, and let us reason together, saith the Lord: though your sins be as scarlet, they shall be as white as snow; though they be red like crimson, they shall be as wool.

Isaiah 1:18

If ye be willing and obedient, ye shall eat the good of the land:

Isaiah 1:19

But they that wait upon the Lord shall renew their strength; they shall mount up with wings as eagles; they shall run, and not be weary; and they shall walk, and not faint.

Isaiah 40:31

Isaiah

Surely he hath borne our griefs, and carried our sorrows: yet we did esteem him stricken, smitten of God, and afflicted.

But he was wounded for our transgressions, he was bruised for our iniquities: the chastisement of our peace was upon him; and with his stripes we are healed.

All we like sheep have gone astray; we have turned every one to his own way; and the Lord hath laid on him the iniquity of us all.

Isaiah 53:4-6

No weapon that is formed against thee shall prosper; and every tongue that shall rise against thee in judgment thou shalt condemn. This is the heritage of the servants of the Lord, and their righteousness is of me, saith the Lord.

Isaiah 54:17

For as the rain cometh down, and the snow from heaven, and returneth not thither, but watereth the earth, and maketh it bring forth and bud, that it may give seed to the sower, and bread to the eater:

So shall my word be that goeth forth out of my mouth: it shall not return unto me void, but it shall accomplish that which I please, and it shall prosper in the thing whereto I sent it.

Isaiah 55:10-11

Behold, the Lord's hand is not shortened, that it cannot save; neither his ear heavy, that it cannot hear:

But your iniquities have separated between you and your God, and your sins have hid his face from you, that he will not hear.

Isaiah 59:1-2

Arise, shine; for thy light is come, and the glory of the Lord is risen upon thee.

Isaiah 60:1

But we are all as an unclean thing, and all our righteousnesses are as filthy rags; and we all do fade as a leaf; and our iniquities, like the wind, have taken us away.

Isaiah 64:6

Before she travailed, she brought forth; before her pain came, she was delivered of a man child.

Isaiah 66:7

Jeremiah

Before I formed thee in the belly I knew thee; and before thou camest forth out of the womb I sanctified thee, and I ordained thee a prophet unto the nations.

Jeremiah 1:5

See, I have this day set thee over the nations and over the kingdoms, to root out, and to pull down, and to destroy, and to throw down, to build, and to plant.

Jeremiah 1:10

And I will give you pastors according to mine heart, which shall feed you with knowledge and understanding.

Jeremiah 3:15

The heart is deceitful above all things, and desperately wicked: who can know it?

Jeremiah 17:9

Heal me, O Lord, and I shall be healed; save me, and I shall be saved: for thou art my praise.

Jeremiah 17:14

Call unto me, and I will answer thee, and show thee great and mighty things, which thou knowest not.

Jeremiah 33:3

Lamentations

It is of the Lord's mercies that we are not consumed, because his compassions fail not.

They are new every morning: great is thy faithfulness.

Lamentations 3:22-23

Who is he that saith, and it cometh to pass, when the Lord commandeth it not?

Lamentations 3:37

Ezekiel

And the spirit entered into me when he spake unto me, and set me upon my feet, that I heard him that spake unto me.

Ezekiel 2:2

Daniel

And such as do wickedly against the covenant shall he corrupt by flatteries: but the people that do know their God shall be strong, and do exploits.

Daniel 11:32

And they that be wise shall shine as the brightness of the firmament; and they that turn many to righteousness as the stars for ever and ever.

Daniel 12:3

Hosea

My people are destroyed for lack of knowledge: because thou hast rejected knowledge, I will also reject thee, that thou shalt be no priest to me: seeing thou hast forgotten the law of thy God, I will also forget thy children.

Hosea 4:6

Amos

Can two walk together, except they be agreed?

Amos 3:3

Micah

Rejoice not against me, O mine enemy: when I fall, I shall arise; when I sit in darkness, the Lord shall be a light unto me.

Micah 7:8

Habakkuk

Although the fig tree shall not blossom, neither shall fruit be in the vines; the labour of the olive shall fail, and the fields shall yield no meat; the flock shall be cut off from the fold, and there shall be no herd in the stalls:

Yet I will rejoice in the Lord, I will joy in the God of my salvation.

Habakkuk 3:17-18

Zephaniah

The Lord thy God in the midst of thee is mighty; he will save, he will rejoice over thee with joy; he will rest in his love, he will joy over thee with singing.

Zephaniah 3:17

Haggai

Ye have sown much, and bring in little; ye eat, but ye have not enough; ye drink, but ye are not filled with drink; ye clothe you, but there is none warm; and he that earneth wages earneth wages to put it into a bag with holes.

Haggai 1:6

Zechariah

Ask ye of the Lord rain in the time of the latter rain; so the Lord shall make bright clouds, and give them showers of rain, to every one grass in the field.

Zechariah 10:1

Matthew

Let your light so shine before men, that they may see your good works, and glorify your Father which is in heaven.

Matthew 5:16

Ask, and it shall be given you; seek, and ye shall find; knock, and it shall be opened unto you:

Matthew 7:7

That it might be fulfilled which was spoken by Esaias the prophet, saying, Himself took our infirmities, and bare our sicknesses.

Matthew 8:17

And Jesus came and spake unto them, saying, All power is given unto me in heaven and in earth.

Go ye therefore, and teach all nations, baptizing them in the name of the Father, and of the Son, and of the Holy Ghost:

Teaching them to observe all things whatsoever I have commanded you: and, lo, I am with you always, even unto the end of the world. Amen.

Matthew 28:18-20

Mark

And Jesus answering saith unto them, Have faith in God.

Mark 11:22

For verily I say unto you, That whosoever shall say unto this mountain, Be thou removed, and be thou cast into the sea; and shall not doubt in his heart, but shall believe that those things which he saith shall come to pass; he shall have whatsoever he saith.

Mark 11:23

Therefore I say unto you, What things soever ye desire, when ye pray, believe that ye receive them, and ye shall have them.

Mark 11:24

And he said unto them, Go ye into all the world, and preach the gospel to every creature.

He that believeth and is baptized shall be saved; but he that believeth not shall be damned.

Mark 16:15-16

And these signs shall follow them that believe; In my name shall they cast out devils; they shall speak with new tongues:

They shall take up serpents; and if they drink any deadly thing, it shall not hurt them; they shall lay hands on the sick, and they shall recover.

Mark 16:17-18

Luke

The Spirit of the Lord is upon me, because he hath anointed me to preach the gospel to the poor; he hath sent me to heal the brokenhearted, to preach deliverance to the captives, and recovering of sight to the blind, to set at liberty them that are bruised:

Luke 4:18

Give, and it shall be given unto you; good measure, pressed down, and shaken together, and running over, shall men give into your bosom. For with the same measure that ye mete withal it shall be measured to you again.

Luke 6:38

And he said unto them, Take heed, and beware of covetousness: for a man's life consisteth not in the abundance of the things which he possesseth.

Luke 12:15

John

as many as received him, to them gave he power to become sons of God, even to them that believe on his name:

John 1:12

That which is born of the flesh is flesh; and that which is born of the Spirit is spirit.

Marvel not that I said unto thee, Ye must be born again.

John 3:6-7

For God so loved the world, that he gave his only begotten Son, that whosoever believeth in him should not perish, but have everlasting life.

For God sent not his Son into the world to condemn the world; but that the world through him might be saved.

John 3:16-17

God is a Spirit: and they that worship him must worship him in spirit and in truth.

John 4:24

It is the spirit that quickeneth; the flesh profiteth nothing: the words that I speak unto you, they are spirit, and they are life.

John 6:63

The thief cometh not, but for to steal, and to kill, and to destroy: I am come that they might have life, and that they might have it more abundantly.

John 10:10

Jesus saith unto him, I am the way, the truth, and the life: no man cometh unto the Father, but by me.

John 14:6

And whatsoever ye shall ask in my name, that will I do, that the Father may be glorified in the Son.

John 14:12

If ye abide in me, and my words abide in you, ye shall ask what ye will, and it shall be done unto you.

John 15:7

Ye have not chosen me, but I have chosen you, and ordained you, that ye should go and bring forth fruit, and that your fruit should remain: that whatsoever ye shall ask of the Father in my name, he may give it you.

John 15:16

John

But when the Comforter is come, whom I will send unto you from the Father, even the Spirit of truth, which proceedeth from the Father, he shall testify of me:

John 15:26

And in that day ye shall ask me nothing. Verily, verily, I say unto you, Whatsoever ye shall ask the Father in my name, he will give it you.

Hitherto have ye asked nothing in my name: ask, and ye shall receive, that your joy may be full.

John 16:23-24

Acts

But ye shall receive power, after that the Holy Ghost is come upon you: and ye shall be witnesses unto me both in Jerusalem, and in all Judaea, and in Samaria, and unto the uttermost part of the earth.

Acts 1:8

And they were all filled with the Holy Ghost, and began to speak with other tongues, as the Spirit gave them utterance.

Acts 2:4

Neither is there salvation in any other: for there is none other name under heaven given among men, whereby we must be saved.

Acts 4:12

How God anointed Jesus of Nazareth with the Holy Ghost and with power: who went about doing good, and healing all that were oppressed of the devil; for God was with him.

Acts 10:38

Take heed therefore unto yourselves, and to all the flock, over the which the Holy Ghost hath made you overseers, to feed the church of God, which he hath purchased with his own blood.

Acts 20:28

Romans

For I am not ashamed of the gospel of Christ: for it is the power of God unto salvation to every one that believeth; to the Jew first, and also to the Greek.

Romans 1:16

Romans

For all have sinned, and come short of the glory of God;

Romans 3:23

For the wages of sin is death; but the gift of God is eternal life through Jesus Christ our Lord.

Romans 6:23

There is therefore now no condemnation to them which are in Christ Jesus, who walk not after the flesh, but after the Spirit.

Romans 8:1

For to be carnally minded is death; but to be spiritually minded is life and peace.

Romans 8:6

For as many as are led by the Spirit of God, they are the sons of God.

Romans 8:14

Likewise the Spirit also helpeth our infirmities: for we know not what we should pray for as we ought: but the

Spirit itself maketh intercession for us with groanings which cannot be uttered.

Romans 8:26

And we know that all things work together for good to them that love God, to them who are the called according to his purpose.

Romans 8:28

That if thou shalt confess with thy mouth the Lord Jesus, and shalt believe in thine heart that God hath raised him from the dead, thou shalt be saved.

For with the heart man believeth unto righteousness; and with the mouth confession is made unto salvation.

Romans 10:9-10

So then faith cometh by hearing, and hearing by the word of God.

Romans 10:17

For the gifts and calling of God are without repentance.

Romans 11:29

Romans

I beseech you therefore, brethren, by the mercies of God, that ye present your bodies a living sacrifice, holy, acceptable unto God, which is your reasonable service.

And be not conformed to this world: but be ye transformed by the renewing of your mind, that ye may prove what is that good, and acceptable, and perfect, will of God.

Romans 12:1-2

Owe no man any thing, but to love one another: for he that loveth another hath fulfilled the law.

Romans 13:8

1 Corinthians

All things are lawful unto me, but all things are not expedient: all things are lawful for me, but I will not be brought under the power of any.

1 Corinthians 6:12

Who goeth a warfare any time at his own charges? who planteth a vineyard, and eateth not of the fruit thereof? or who feedeth a flock, and eateth not of the milk of the flock?

1 Corinthians 9:7

There hath no temptation taken you but such as is common to man: but God is faithful, who will not suffer you to be tempted above that ye are able; but will with the temptation also make a way to escape, that ye may be able to bear it.

1 Corinthians 10:13

All things are lawful for me, but all things are not expedient: all things are lawful for me, but all things edify not.

1 Corinthians 10:23

But the manifestation of the Spirit is given to every man to profit withal.

1 Corinthians 12:7

1 Corinthians

Charity suffereth long, and is kind; charity envieth not; charity vaunteth not itself, is not puffed up, Doth not behave itself unseemly, seeketh not her own, is not easily provoked, thinketh no evil; Rejoiceth not in iniquity, but rejoiceth in the truth;

Beareth all things, believeth all things, hopeth all things, endureth all things.

1 Corinthians 13:4-7

Follow after charity, and desire spiritual gifts, but rather that ye may prophesy.

For he that speaketh in an unknown tongue speaketh not unto men, but unto God: for no man understandeth him; howbeit in the spirit he speaketh mysteries.

But he that prophesieth speaketh unto men to edification, and exhortation, and comfort.

1 Corinthians 14:1-2

But he that prophesieth speaketh unto men to edification, and exhortation, and comfort. He that speaketh in an unknown tongue edifieth himself; but he that prophesieth edifieth the church.

1 Corinthians 14:3-4

There are, it may be, so many kinds of voices in the world, and none of them is without signification.

> 1 Corinthians 14:10

For if I pray in an unknown tongue, my spirit prayeth, but my understanding is unfruitful.

What is it then? I will pray with the spirit, and I will pray with the understanding also: I will sing with the spirit, and I will sing with the understanding also.

> 1 Corinthians 14:14-15

1 Corinthians

Be not deceived: evil communications corrupt good manners.

> 1 Corinthians 15:33

Therefore, my beloved brethren, be ye stedfast, unmoveable, always abounding in the work of the Lord, forasmuch as ye know that your labour is not in vain in the Lord.

> 1 Corinthians 15:58

2 Corinthians

When I therefore was thus minded, did I use lightness? or the things that I purpose, do I purpose according to the flesh, that with me there should be yea yea, and nay nay?

> 2 Corinthians 1:17

Now thanks be unto God, which always causeth us to triumph in Christ, and maketh manifest the savour of his knowledge by us in every place.

2 Corinthians 2:14

Now the Lord is that Spirit: and where the Spirit of the Lord is, there is liberty.

2 Corinthians 3:17

But if our gospel be hid, it is hid to them that are lost:

2 Corinthians 4:3

In whom the god of this world hath blinded the minds of them which believe not, lest the light of the glorious gospel of Christ, who is the image of God, should shine unto them.

2 Corinthians 4:4

We having the same spirit of faith, according as it is written, I believed, and therefore have I spoken; we also believe, and therefore speak;

2 Corinthians 4:13

For which cause we faint not; but though our outward man perish, yet the inward man is renewed day by day.

For our light affliction, which is but for a moment, worketh for us a far more exceeding and eternal weight of glory;

2 Corinthians 4:16-17

2 Corinthians

While we look not at the things which are seen, but at the things which are not seen: for the things which are seen are temporal; but the things which are not seen are eternal.

2 Corinthians 4:18

For we know that if our earthly house of this tabernacle were dissolved, we have a building of God, an house not made with hands, eternal in the heavens.

For in this we groan, earnestly desiring to be clothed upon with our house which is from heaven:

2 Corinthians 5:1-2

(For we walk by faith, not by sight:)

2 Corinthians 5:7

For we must all appear before the judgment seat of Christ; that every one may receive the things done in his body, according to that he hath done, whether it be good or bad.

2 Corinthians 5:10

For the love of Christ constraineth us; because we thus judge, that if one died for all, then were all dead:

And that he died for all, that they which live should not henceforth live unto themselves, but unto him which died for them, and rose again.

2 Corinthians 5:14-15

Therefore if any man be in Christ, he is a new creature: old things are passed away; behold, all things are become new.

2 Corinthians 5:17

Be ye not unequally yoked together with unbelievers: for what fellowship hath righteousness with unrighteousness? and what communion hath light with darkness?

2 Corinthians 6:14

For ye know the grace of our Lord Jesus Christ, that, though he was rich, yet for your sakes he became poor, that ye through his poverty might be rich.

2 Corinthians 8:9

2 Corinthians

But this I say, He which soweth sparingly shall reap also sparingly; and he which soweth bountifully shall reap also bountifully.

Every man according as he purposeth in his heart, so let him give; not grudgingly, or of necessity: for God loveth a cheerful giver.

And God is able to make all grace abound toward you; that ye, always having all sufficiency in all things, may abound to every good work:

2 Corinthians 9:6-8

(For the weapons of our warfare are not carnal, but mighty through God to the pulling down of strong holds;)

Casting down imaginations, and every high thing that exalteth itself against the knowledge of God, and bringing into captivity every thought to the obedience of Christ;

And having in a readiness to revenge all disobedience, when your obedience is fulfilled.

2 Corinthians 10:4-6

And he said unto me, My grace is sufficient for thee: for my strength is made perfect in weakness. Most gladly therefore will I rather glory in my infirmities, that the power of Christ may rest upon me.

Therefore I take pleasure in infirmities, in reproaches, in necessities, in persecutions, in distresses for Christ's sake: for when I am weak, then am I strong.

2 Corinthians 12:9-10

Examine yourselves, whether ye be in the faith; prove your own selves. Know ye not your own selves, how that Jesus Christ is in you, except ye be reprobates?

2 Corinthians 13:5

Galatians

For do I now persuade men, or God? or do I seek to please men? for if I yet pleased men, I should not be the servant of Christ.

Galatians 1:10

For if I build again the things which I destroyed, I make myself a transgressor.

Galatians 2:18

I am crucified with Christ: nevertheless I live; yet not I, but Christ liveth in me: and the life which I now live in the flesh I live by the faith of the Son of God, who loved me, and gave himself for me.

Galatians 2:20

Christ hath redeemed us from the curse of the law, being made a curse for us: for it is written, Cursed is every one that hangeth on a tree:

That the blessing of Abraham might come on the Gentiles through Jesus Christ; that we might receive the promise of the Spirit through faith.

Galatians 3:13-14

There is neither Jew nor Greek, there is neither bond nor free, there is neither male nor female: for ye are all one in Christ Jesus.

Galatians 3:28

Am I therefore become your enemy, because I tell you the truth?

Galatians 4:16

But it is good to be zealously affected always in a good thing, and not only when I am present with you.

Galatians 4:18

My little children, of whom I travail in birth again until Christ be formed in you.

Galatians 4:19

Stand fast therefore in the liberty wherewith Christ hath made us free, and be not entangled again with the yoke of bondage.

Galatians 5:1

A little leaven leaveneth the whole lump.

Galatians 5:9

This I say then, Walk in the Spirit, and ye shall not fulfil the lust of the flesh.

For the flesh lusteth against the Spirit, and the Spirit against the flesh: and these are contrary the one to the other: so that ye cannot do the things that ye would.

Galatians 5:16-17

Galatians

Now the works of the flesh are manifest, which are these; Adultery, fornication, uncleanness, lasciviousness,

Idolatry, witchcraft, hatred, variance, emulations, wrath, strife, seditions, heresies,

Envyings, murders, drunkenness, revellings, and such like: of the which I tell you before, as I have also told you in time past, that they which do such things shall not inherit the kingdom of God.

Galatians 5:19-21

But the fruit of the Spirit is love, joy, peace, longsuffering, gentleness, goodness, faith, Meekness, temperance: against such there is no law.

Galatians 5:22-23

Brethren, if a man be overtaken in a fault, ye which are spiritual, restore such an one in the spirit of meekness; considering thyself, lest thou also be tempted.

Galatians 6:1

Let him that is taught in the word communicate unto him that teacheth in all good things.

Galatians 6:6

Be not deceived; God is not mocked: for whatsoever a man soweth, that shall he also reap.

For he that soweth to his flesh shall of the flesh reap corruption; but he that soweth to the Spirit shall of the Spirit reap life everlasting.

Galatians 6:7-8

And let us not be weary in well doing: for in due season we shall reap, if we faint not.

As we have therefore opportunity, let us do good unto all men, especially unto them who are of the household of faith.

Galatians 6:9-10

Ephesians

That the God of our Lord Jesus Christ, the Father of glory, may give unto you the spirit of wisdom and revelation in the knowledge of him:

Ephesians 1:17

And you hath he quickened, who were dead in trespasses and sins; Wherein in time past ye walked according to the course of this world, according to the prince of the power of the air, the spirit that now worketh in the children of disobedience:

Ephesians 2:1-2

For we are his workmanship, created in Christ Jesus unto good works, which God hath before ordained that we should walk in them.

Ephesians 2:10

Now unto him that is able to do exceeding abundantly above all that we ask or think, according to the power that worketh in us,

Unto him be glory in the church by Christ Jesus throughout all ages, world without end. Amen.

Ephesians 3:20-21

And he gave some, apostles; and some, prophets; and some, evangelists; and some, pastors and teachers;

Ephesians 4:11

For the perfecting of the saints, for the work of the ministry, for the edifying of the body of Christ:

Ephesians 4:12

Till we all come in the unity of the faith, and of the knowledge of the Son of God, unto a perfect man, unto the measure of the stature of the fulness of Christ:

That we henceforth be no more children, tossed to and fro, and carried about with every wind of doctrine, by the sleight of men, and cunning craftiness, whereby they lie in wait to deceive;

Ephesians 4:13-14

Be ye angry, and sin not: let not the sun go down upon your wrath:

Ephesians 4:26

Neither give place to the devil.

Ephesians 4:27

Ephesians

Let no corrupt communication proceed out of your mouth, but that which is good to the use of edifying, that it may minister grace unto the hearers.

Ephesians 4:29

And grieve not the holy Spirit of God, whereby ye are sealed unto the day of redemption.

Ephesians 4:30

Be ye therefore followers of God, as dear children;

Ephesians 5:1

And walk in love, as Christ also hath loved us, and hath given himself for us an offering and a sacrifice to God for a sweetsmelling savour.

Ephesians 5:2

But fornication, and all uncleanness, or covetousness, let it not be once named among you, as becometh saints;

Ephesians 5:3

Redeeming the time, because the days are evil.

Ephesians 5:16

And be not drunk with wine, wherein is excess; but be filled with the Spirit; Speaking to yourselves in psalms and hymns and spiritual songs, singing and making melody in your heart to the Lord;

Ephesians 5:18-19

Wives, submit yourselves unto your own husbands, as unto the Lord.

Ephesians 5:22

Honour thy father and mother; which is the first commandment with promise;

That it may be well with thee, and thou mayest live long on the earth.

Ephesians 6:2-3

Finally, my brethren, be strong in the Lord, and in the power of his might.

Ephesians 6:10

Put on the whole armour of God, that ye may be able to stand against the wiles of the devil.

Ephesians 6:11

For we wrestle not against flesh and blood, but against principalities, against powers, against the rulers of the darkness of this world, against spiritual wickedness in high places.

Ephesians 6:12

Ephesians

Praying always with all prayer and supplication in the Spirit, and watching thereunto with all perseverance and supplication for all saints;

Ephesians 6:18

Philippians

For to me to live is Christ, and to die is gain.

Philippians 1:21

And in nothing terrified by your adversaries: which is to them an evident token of perdition, but to you of salvation, and that of God.

For unto you it is given in the behalf of Christ, not only to believe on him, but also to suffer for his sake;

Philippians 1:28-29

Let nothing be done through strife or vainglory; but in lowliness of mind let each esteem other better than themselves.

Philippians 2:3

That at the name of Jesus every knee should bow, of things in heaven, and things in earth, and things under the earth;

Philippians 2:10

Wherefore, my beloved, as ye have always obeyed, not as in my presence only, but now much more in my absence, work out your own salvation with fear and trembling.

Philippians 2:12

For I have no man likeminded, who will naturally care for your state.

For all seek their own, not the things which are Jesus Christ's.

Philippians 2:20-21

That I may know him, and the power of his resurrection, and the fellowship of his sufferings, being made conformable unto his death;

Philippians 3:10

Brethren, I count not myself to have apprehended: but this one thing I do, forgetting those things which are behind, and reaching forth unto those things which are before,

I press toward the mark for the prize of the high calling of God in Christ Jesus.

Philippians 3:13-14

Philippians

Be careful for nothing; but in every thing by prayer and supplication with thanksgiving let your requests be made known unto God.

Philippians 4:6

Finally, brethren, whatsoever things are true, whatsoever things are honest, whatsoever things are just, whatsoever things are pure, whatsoever things are lovely, whatsoever things are of good report; if there be any virtue, and if there be any praise, think on these things.

Philippians 4:8

I can do all things through Christ which strengtheneth me.

Philippians 4:13

But my God shall supply all your need according to his riches in glory by Christ Jesus.

Philippians 4:19

Colossians

Who hath delivered us from the power of darkness, and hath translated us into the kingdom of his dear Son:

Colossians 1:13

Let the word of Christ dwell in you richly in all wisdom; teaching and admonishing one another in psalms and hymns and spiritual songs, singing with grace in your hearts to the Lord.

Colossians 3:16

1 Thessalonians

For the Lord himself shall descend from heaven with a shout, with the voice of the archangel, and with the trump of God: and the dead in Christ shall rise first:

Then we which are alive and remain shall be caught up together with them in the clouds, to meet the Lord in the air: and so shall we ever be with the Lord.

Wherefore comfort one another with these words.

1 Thessalonians 4:16-18

1 Thessalonians

Rejoice evermore.

1 Thessalonians 5:16

Pray without ceasing.

1 Thessalonians 5:17

In every thing give thanks: for this is the will of God in Christ Jesus concerning you.

1 Thessalonians 5:18

Quench not the Spirit.

1 Thessalonians 5:19

Despise not prophesyings.

1 Thessalonians 5:20

Prove all things; hold fast that which is good.

1 Thessalonians 5:21

Abstain from all appearance of evil.

1 Thessalonians 5:22

And the very God of peace sanctify you wholly; and I pray God your whole spirit and soul and body be preserved blameless unto the coming of our Lord Jesus Christ.

1 Thessalonians 5:23

1 Timothy

I exhort therefore, that, first of all, supplications, prayers, intercessions, and giving of thanks, be made for all men;

For kings, and for all that are in authority; that we may lead a quiet and peaceable life in all godliness and honesty.

1 Timothy 2:1-2

1 Timothy

For there is one God, and one mediator between God and men, the man Christ Jesus;

1 Timothy 2:5

This is a true saying, if a man desire the office of a bishop, he desireth a good work.

1 Timothy 3:1

Neglect not the gift that is in thee, which was given thee by prophecy, with the laying on of the hands of the presbytery. Meditate upon these things; give thyself wholly to them; that thy profiting may appear to all.

1 Timothy 4:14-15

Take heed unto thyself, and unto the doctrine; continue in them: for in doing this thou shalt both save thyself, and them that hear thee.

1 Timothy 4:16

But godliness with contentment is great gain.

For we brought nothing into this world, and it is certain we can carry nothing out.

And having food and raiment let us be therewith content.

1 Timothy 6: 6-8

For the love of money is the root of all evil: which while some coveted after, they have erred from the faith, and pierced themselves through with many sorrows.

1 Timothy 6:10

Fight the good fight of faith, lay hold on eternal life, whereunto thou art also called, and hast professed a good profession before many witnesses.

1 Timothy 6:12

2 Timothy

Thou therefore, my son, be strong in the grace that is in Christ Jesus.

And the things that thou hast heard of me among many witnesses, the same commit thou to faithful men, who shall be able to teach others also.

2 Timothy 2:1-2

Thou therefore endure hardness, as a good soldier of Jesus Christ.

No man that warreth entangleth himself with the affairs of this life; that he may please him who hath chosen him to be a soldier.

2 Timothy 2:3-4

2 Timothy

Study to shew thyself approved unto God, a workman that needeth not to be ashamed, rightly dividing the word of truth.

2 Timothy 2:15

Nevertheless the foundation of God standeth sure, having this seal, The Lord knoweth them that are his. And, let every one that nameth the name of Christ depart from iniquity.

2 Timothy 2:19

But in a great house there are not only vessels of gold and of silver, but also of wood and of earth; and some to honour, and some to dishonour.

2 Timothy 2:20

All scripture is given by inspiration of God, and is profitable for doctrine, for reproof, for correction, for instruction in righteousness:

That the man of God may be perfect, thoroughly furnished unto all good works.

2 Timothy 3:16-17

Titus

For the grace of God that bringeth salvation hath appeared to all men,

Teaching us that, denying ungodliness and worldly lusts, we should live soberly, righteously, and godly, in this present world;

Titus 2:11-12

Philemon

That the communication of thy faith may become effectual by the acknowledging of every good thing which is in you in Christ Jesus.

Philemon 1:6

Hebrews

How shall we escape, if we neglect so great salvation; which at the first began to be spoken by the Lord, and was confirmed unto us by them that heard him;

Hebrews 2:3

Hebrews

For unto us was the gospel preached, as well as unto them: but the word preached did not profit them, not being mixed with faith in them that heard it.

Hebrews 4:2

For the word of God is quick, and powerful, and sharper than any twoedged sword, piercing even to the dividing asunder of soul and spirit, and of the joints and marrow, and is a discerner of the thoughts and intents of the heart.

Hebrews 4:12

Let us therefore come boldly unto the throne of grace, that we may obtain mercy, and find grace to help in time of need.

Hebrews 4:16

Who in the days of his flesh, when he had offered up prayers and supplications with strong crying and tears unto him that was able to save him from death, and was heard in that he feared;

Hebrews 5:7

For when for the time ye ought to be teachers, ye have need that one teach you again which be the first principles of the oracles of God; and are become such as have need of milk, and not of strong meat.

For every one that useth milk is unskilful in the word of righteousness: for he is a babe.

But strong meat belongeth to them that are of full age, even those who by reason of use have their senses exercised to discern both good and evil.

Hebrews 5:12-14

Therefore leaving the principles of the doctrine of Christ, let us go on unto perfection; not laying again the foundation of repentance from dead works, and of faith toward God,

Of the doctrine of baptisms, and of laying on of hands, and of resurrection of the dead, and of eternal judgment.

Hebrews 6:1-2

That ye be not slothful, but followers of them who through faith and patience inherit the promises.

Hebrews 6:12

And almost all things are by the law purged with blood; and without shedding of blood is no remission.

Hebrews 9:22

Hebrews

And as it is appointed unto men once to die, but after this the judgment:

Hebrews 9:27

Not forsaking the assembling of ourselves together, as the manner of some is; but exhorting one another: and so much the more, as ye see the day approaching.

Hebrews 10:25

Now the just shall live by faith: but if any man draw back, my soul shall have no pleasure in him.

Hebrews 10:38

Now faith is the substance of things hoped for, the evidence of things not seen.

Hebrews 11:1

But without faith it is impossible to please him: for he that cometh to God must believe that he is, and that he is a rewarder of them that diligently seek him.

Hebrews 11:6

Wherefore seeing we also are compassed about with so great a cloud of witnesses, let us lay aside every weight, and the sin which doth so easily beset us, and let us run with patience the race that is set before us,

Looking unto Jesus the author and finisher of our faith; who for the joy that was set before him endured the cross, despising the shame, and is set down at the right hand of the throne of God.

Hebrews 12:1-2

For whom the Lord loveth he chasteneth, and scourgeth every son whom he receiveth.

Hebrews 12:6

Follow peace with all men, and holiness, without which no man shall see the Lord:

Looking diligently lest any man fail of the grace of God; lest any root of bitterness springing up trouble you, and thereby many be defiled;

Hebrews 12:14-15

Let brotherly love continue.

Hebrews 13:1

Hebrews

Marriage is honourable in all, and the bed undefiled: but whoremongers and adulterers God will judge.

Let your conversation be without covetousness; and be content with such things as ye have: for he hath said, I will never leave thee, nor forsake thee.

Hebrews 13:4-5

Jesus Christ the same yesterday, and to day, and for ever.

Hebrews 13:8

Obey them that have the rule over you, and submit yourselves: for they watch for your souls, as they that must give account, that they may do it with joy, and not with grief: for that is unprofitable for you.

Hebrews 13:17

James

If any of you lack wisdom, let him ask of God, that giveth to all men liberally, and upbraideth not; and it shall be given him.

James 1:5

A double minded man is unstable in all his ways.

James 1:8

Let no man say when he is tempted, I am tempted of God: for God cannot be tempted with evil, neither tempteth he any man: But every man is tempted, when he is drawn away of his own lust, and enticed.

James 1:13-14

Every good gift and every perfect gift is from above, and cometh down from the Father of lights, with whom is no variableness, neither shadow of turning.

James 1:17

For whosoever shall keep the whole law, and yet offend in one point, he is guilty of all.

James 2:10

Even so faith, if it hath not works, is dead, being alone.

James 2:17

James

But the wisdom that is from above is first pure, then peaceable, gentle, and easy to be intreated, full of mercy and good fruits, without partiality, and without hypocrisy.

James 3:17

Ye adulterers and adulteresses, know ye not that the friendship of the world is enmity with God? whosoever therefore will be a friend of the world is the enemy of God.

James 4:4

Submit yourselves therefore to God. Resist the devil, and he will flee from you.

James 4:7

Humble yourselves in the sight of the Lord, and he shall lift you up.

James 4:10

Confess your faults one to another, and pray one for another, that ye may be healed. The effectual fervent prayer of a righteous man availeth much.

James 5:16

1 Peter

As newborn babes, desire the sincere milk of the word, that ye may grow thereby:

1 Peter 2:2

To whom coming, as unto a living stone, disallowed indeed of men, but chosen of God, and precious,

1 Peter 2:4

But ye are a chosen generation, a royal priesthood, an holy nation, a peculiar people; that ye should shew forth the praises of him who hath called you out of darkness into his marvellous light;

1 Peter 2:9

Who his own self bare our sins in his own body on the tree, that we, being dead to sins, should live unto righteousness: by whose stripes ye were healed.

1 Peter 2:24

The elders which are among you I exhort, who am also an elder, and a witness of the sufferings of Christ, and also a partaker of the glory that shall be revealed:

Feed the flock of God which is among you, taking the oversight thereof, not by constraint, but willingly; not for filthy lucre, but of a ready mind;

1 Peter 5:1-2

1 Peter

Casting all your care upon him; for he careth for you.

Be sober, be vigilant; because your adversary the devil, as a roaring lion, walketh about, seeking whom he may devour:

1 Peter 5:7-8

2 Peter

Knowing this first, that no prophecy of the scripture is of any private interpretation.

2 Peter 1:20

For the prophecy came not in old time by the will of man: but holy men of God spake as they were moved by the Holy Ghost.

2 Peter 1:21

1 John

If we say that we have no sin, we deceive ourselves, and the truth is not in us.

If we confess our sins, he is faithful and just to forgive us our sins, and to cleanse us from all unrighteousness.

1 John 1:8-9

Love not the world, neither the things that are in the world. If any man love the world, the love of the Father is not in him.

1 John 2:15

Little children, let no man deceive you: he that doeth righteousness is righteous, even as he is righteous.

1 John 3:7

Ye are of God, little children, and have overcome them: because greater is he that is in you, than he that is in the world.

1 John 4:4

Beloved, let us love one another: for love is of God; and every one that loveth is born of God, and knoweth God.

1 John 4:7

For whatsoever is born of God overcometh the world: and this is the victory that overcometh the world, even our faith.

1 John 5:4

1 John

And this is the confidence that we have in him, that, if we ask any thing according to his will, he heareth us:

And if we know that he hear us, whatsoever we ask, we know that we have the petitions that we desired of him.

1 John 5:14-15

3 John

Beloved, I wish above all things that thou mayest prosper and be in health, even as thy soul prospereth.

3 John 1:2

Jude

But ye, beloved, building up yourselves on your most holy faith, praying in the Holy Ghost,

Jude 1:20

Revelation

Behold, I stand at the door, and knock: if any man hear my voice, and open the door, I will come in to him, and will sup with him, and he with me.

Revelation 3:20

Prayer of salvation

If you have read this book and you want to surrender your life to Jesus Christ today, please say this prayer.

My Father in heaven, I recognise that I am a sinner.

I recognise that the Lord Jesus died for me and paid

the penalty for my sins.

Dear Lord, today, I repent of my sins and I accept

Jesus Christ as my Lord and Saviour.

Wash me with your blood and make me holy.

Please write my name in the book of life and give me

the grace to serve you.

Thank you that I am born again.

AMEN

prayer and you believe it in your heart, you
a new creation in Christ! Congratulations! I
bible believing church where the solid word
and attend regularly. God bless you.

Other titles by Ernest Add

THE FOUNDATIONS OF TRUE FAITH

The Christian walk is all about FAITH. Many people put their faith in worldly things, philosophies and idols. Discover the True Faith which is Jesus Christ! This book will teach you about The Foundations of True Faith. In it, you will discover:

- *The revelation of who Faith is*

- *The Power of Faith and how to activate it*

- *How to identify the Enemies of Faith*

- *The Types of Faith*

- *The importance of the Pillars of Faith*

- *How to build your Faith*

This book is essential reading to help you develop a strong faith in Jesus Christ. Written with practical examples, testimonies and biblical truths, it will help you to stand firm in Christ no matter the storm!